Field conditions at Soos Park Field prior to start of championship game, June 11, 1960. *Photo extracted from 8mm film taken by Harold McCracken, father of utility second baseman Jerry McCracken.*

Rain Delayed

A Personal and Collective Recount of the Whitworth Pirates' Journey Through the NAIA Baseball Tournament in Sioux City, Iowa: June, 1960

LINDA MERKEL WALLINE

authorHOUSE®

AuthorHouse™
1663 Liberty Drive
Bloomington, IN 47403
www.authorhouse.com
Phone: 1-800-839-8640

Published by AuthorHouse 5/2/2013

ISBN: 978-1-4817-4339-6 (sc)
ISBN: 978-1-4817-4338-9 (e)

Library of Congress Control Number: 2013907443

Any people depicted in stock imagery provided by Thinkstock are models, and such images are being used for illustrative purposes only. Certain stock imagery © Thinkstock.

This book is printed on acid-free paper.

Table of Contents

Prologue: Creating A Champion

The year was 1960. My father, Paul Merkel, was thirty-eight years old and head baseball coach at Whitworth College (now Whitworth University). He had been head coach since the spring of 1956. During that time, Dad also assisted with the football backfield, served as athletic director, and filled in with any sport that needed his assistance. Whatever needed doing, my father did it. But baseball was his passion, and his ballplayers were family.

Whitworth is a small Christian college nestled among pine trees, just north of the city of Spokane, Washington. Like many small private colleges, Whitworth had struggled for years following World War II to finance its various athletic programs. In fact, baseball hadn't been reintroduced until 1948, the first time since 1935 Whitworth fielded an intercollegiate baseball team.

Those of us in "Coach Merkel's" family always knew that baseball was part of my father's soul, but we didn't find out until years after his retirement that Dad had been a talented baseball player in his own right, catching for both his high school team and for a local recreation league team in Sprague, Washington. He was good enough that he had his eye on obtaining a baseball scholarship from Washington State University, anticipating that a successful stint at WSU would provide his best opportunity to one day play professional ball. He initiated contact with the head coach and sent letters of reference, including an impressive tally of his accomplishments and leadership positions throughout high school. His efforts were rewarded with an offer to play for the Cougars. I can imagine the elation he must have felt when he signed that letter of intent, realizing his dream to play ball on the collegiate level. But my father had underestimated the strength of purpose with which his mother, a fundamentalist Christian widow and stern disciplinarian, approached the idea of her son attending college. She had forbidden him to play on any summer league team sponsored by a town tavern and had no intention of permitting her son to attend a state university, athletic scholarship or not. No, Whitworth was the college she had chosen for him; the fact that Whitworth did not have a baseball program in 1940 did little to deter her resolve.

My father loved and respected his mother and was not given to going against her will. His father had died when he was barely twelve years old, leaving him, his mother, and his baby sister to manage their large wheat ranch located between Sprague and Edwall. Ever mindful of the temptations surrounding a young man who was growing up without the advantage of a guiding male figure in his life, Lena Merkel compensated by maintaining strict control over her son's activities. And so, he turned down the scholarship and the chance to play baseball at WSU and became a freshman at Whitworth College in 1940. I wondered if it didn't break his heart a little to give up the chance to play the sport he loved so dearly on a collegiate level. But if that disappointment did break his heart, he did not let it break his spirit. Over the next three years my father filled the gap by successfully pursuing letters in football, basketball, and tennis.

In 1943, his college career was interrupted by a call to serve his country in World War II. He chose to enlist in the navy. After basic training he went on to Chicago, where he completed the officer training program at Northwestern University.

Having grown to love Whitworth during his previous three years as a student and feeling secure in its Christian atmosphere, Dad chose to return in 1946 after serving his time in the Pacific as a naval lieutenant. This time around, however, he was older and no longer content to yield to the status quo. With the single-minded determination he later displayed as a coach and mentor, he became instrumental in rebuilding Whitworth's baseball program. At first he served as a graduate assistant in both basketball and football, but finally, in 1948, Whitworth administrators gave the nod to expand the athletic department to include intercollegiate baseball.

My mother (also a Whitworth alum) and father were married in 1947, a few months after graduation. My mother was as artistic as my father was athletic, but she had grown up in the small mining community of Mullan, Idaho, and appreciated all kinds of outdoor activities, whether it was fishing, hiking, skiing, or baseball. My father always said that it was my mom who pursued and caught him. I never believed that for a moment.

Newly married and in need of a paying job, Dad jumped at the opportunity to teach and coach at his high school alma mater in Sprague, Washington. He was there for four years before accepting a similar position in Tonasket. However, his years coaching high school athletics proved unexpectedly stressful, both professionally and personally. In 1954, remembering both Whitworth's fledgling baseball program and the structure and spiritual stability he found at the small Christian college, he decided that the time was right to pursue his masters degree in education, and the natural choice was to do so at Whitworth. It was with that intention that he and my mother packed up their belongings and their three young daughters and returned to Spokane. To help finance his degree program, Dad was given the opportunity to serve as a graduate assistant and later as an assistant coach in football, basketball, and baseball. His first contract of employment at Whitworth specified a whopping annual compensation of $3,450, payable in twelve equal installments. When baseball coach Art Smith resigned in 1956, my father took over as head coach. Three years later, the Whitworth Pirate baseball team enjoyed its first Evergreen Conference Championship.

Historically, 1960 was a pivotal year for the country as well as for athletics. It was a year that saw the first televised Olympic Games (including the US hockey team's improbable win over Czechoslovakia for a gold medal), Ted Williams' 500th home run, and the expansion of professional football to include teams from Dallas and Oakland. But

1960 also ushered in a period of unrest and disillusionment, reflected in literature like *Catch 22*, *To Kill a Mockingbird*, and *The Feminine Mystique*. Students were taking to the streets, demonstrating in Atlanta churches and staging sit-ins at colleges around the country to promote their push for civil rights, women's liberation, and equality. John F. Kennedy was running for president, OPEC was formed by oil-exporting countries in the Middle East, and the USS *Enterprise* was launched as the first nuclear-powered aircraft carrier.

It was in this setting that my father, Coach Paul Merkel, fielded his 1960 baseball team.

Whitworth Baseball Team – spring 1960. *Photo reprinted courtesy of Whitworth University Archives.*

Whitworth Baseball Team Roster
June 1960

Name	No.	Position	Year Graduated	Home Town
Walter (Spike) Grosvenor	13	Pitcher	1963	Spokane, WA
Bill Trenbeath	3	2nd Base	1963	Neche, ND
Jerry McCracken	15	2nd Base	1962	Denver, CO
Don Cox	12	2nd Base	1963	Spokane, WA
Lee Archer	7	Center Field	1962	Alameda, CA
Tom Ingram	6	Pitcher	1962	Yakima, WA
Dean McGuire	14	3rd Base	1961	Colorado Springs, CO
Jim Glennon	8	Catcher	1960	Emmett, ID
Farrell Romig	5	Outfield	1961	Spokane, WA
Norm Harding	2	Shortstop	1962	Spokane, WA
Dennis (Denny) Rieger	10	Catcher	1962	Ritzville, WA
Abe Roberts	9	First Base	1962	Deer Park, WA
Bob Huber	21	Pitcher	1962	Los Angeles, CA
Jerry Breymeyer	20	First Base	1961	Naches, WA
Ray Washburn	24	Pitcher	1961	Burbank, WA
Ron Lince	16	Outfield	1960	Selah, WA
Dale Roberts	4	Pitcher	1961	Riverside, WA
Ken Wittenburg		Ass't. Coach	1959	Castle Rock, WA
Paul Merkel	22	Head Coach	1947	Sprague, WA

1:
Rain Delay

Rain delay. Just minutes before, the grandstands had hosted a cadre of NAIA officials and spectators willing to brave the elements to watch the championship game. Now those same grandstands stood motionless against the elemental onslaught, their previous tenants having abandoned their vigil and retreated to drier locales. Ballplayers from both teams held their ground, huddling in their respective dugouts … to wait. And wait they would. It was the biggest game of their lives. They weren't going anywhere until a winner was determined.

2:

Spring Fever

Wind and rain defined most of Whitworth's 1960 baseball season, dating back to early April. The Pirates hadn't gotten outside to practice or to scrimmage as a team, nor had their pitchers thrown a single pitch off the mound, before they headed to Seattle for their first games that spring. When they did hit the road, their coach, my father, wasn't with them. Instead, Ross Cutter, the newly hired men's tennis coach, stepped in and accompanied the team on their first road trip.

Ross was an energetic sprite of a man, a California native, much more acclimated to the warmth and sunshine of the Bay area than the cold dampness of a Washington spring. He made quite a spectacle. His long black rain coat flapped like a landlocked raven in the unrelenting wind and rain as he paced outside the dugout or around the third base coach's box, his oversized galoshes providing further testament to his discomfiture on the field. Not wanting to appear totally useless, Coach Cutter had flapped out to the pitcher's mound during one of those first games when it appeared that Spike Grosvenor, Whitworth's young starting pitcher, was losing control.

"Are you worried, son?" he asked Spike.

"I'm okay, but...," the end of his thought trailed off as Spike kicked the rubber and cast an anxious glance toward the opponents on base.

"Hmmmm, well, the seven of us on the bench are mighty worried," Coach Cutter proclaimed as he turned and flapped back to the visitors' dugout, leaving Spike to work his own way out of a bases-loaded jam. And all the while, my father remained homebound.

Dad had spent much of February and March in bed with pneumonia. It was a tough case from the beginning, probably because the coach didn't know how to "take it easy." Finally, he was given no choice. I remember those days and weeks clearly; he on the couch in the living room while I or my two younger sisters entertained him or sat with him in front of the old black-and-white television set, watching variety shows or whatever else happened to be broadcasting. But he lived for the news, when he could catch up on the scores and highlights from games and sports that were not adequately covered by our local newspaper. In those days, the *Spokesman Review's* sports page was just that—a page, two at most.

Not being the most compliant patient and wanting desperately to be on the field with his players, it was necessary to find an activity to occupy both my Dad's mind and his time while he was virtually bedridden. That activity turned out to be stamp collecting. I was ten years old at the time, and being the eldest, it was an endeavor that I was able to share with him. I reveled in every minute of it. Professors and administrators at Whitworth would save stamps off of envelopes coming from all over the world and package them up for delivery through the campus mail. At home, we would open bulging manila envelopes containing hundreds of stamps of every denomination and every color; from countries I hadn't even read about in school. He would pick out the stamps he wanted to mount in his massive collection book and, with feelings of great importance, I would take them to the bathroom and soak them carefully in the sink or bathtub until the stamps pulled away from the envelope to which they adhered. As the stamps dried on towels spread out over the bathroom floor, I carefully kept them flat and unharmed until I returned them to my Dad to mount in his stamp book. It was, perhaps, a poor substitute for being at baseball practice and accompanying the team on their first road trip, but sharing that kind of time with the coach was unusual for me, and once he regained his health, it was an occasion that never happened again.

***

April and May had come and gone. It was June now and the third inning of the championship game had just reached a soggy conclusion. My father had returned to the baseball field a little over two and half months ago and now everything was at a standstill, waiting for the rain to recede enough for play to continue. Pitchers for both Whitworth and Georgia Southern were in their respective dugouts, desperately trying to keep their arms warm. Sioux City, typically hot and sticky that time of year, had been unusually wet during the last three days of the NAIA National Intercollegiate Baseball Championship. In fact, rain had punctuated play throughout most of the loser-out game the day before, as well. You had to give credit to NAIA officials and to the groundskeepers; they tried everything they could to keep the infields playable at Soos Park Ball Field, including an attempt to hover a helicopter over the field, hoping that, if nothing else, the rotor action would dissipate the larger pools of water. Today, Championship Saturday, the infield was still plagued with standing water, the base paths were muddy and treacherous, the outfield was sodden. Earlier in the morning, as soon as a break in the clouds was spotted, the field crew poured gasoline on the base paths, torching the volatile fluid to help burn off some of the standing water in anticipation of the first pitch. It may have smelled bad, but the technique, while inherently dangerous for those tossing the matches, worked surprisingly well.:

Under ordinary circumstances, officials probably would have rescheduled the game for another day. But this was the championship game, and both teams were under strict deadlines for returning home. There was nothing left to do but wait out the gloom and hope for enough daylight to finish the game.

Soos Park grounds crew lighting gasoline along base paths to burn off standing water. *Photo extracted from 8 mm film taken by Harold McCracken, father of utility second baseman Jerry McCracken.*

Soos Park grounds crew lighting gasoline along base paths to burn off standing water. *Photo extracted from 8 mm film taken by Harold McCracken, father of utility second baseman Jerry McCracken.*

3:
Ticket Punched

What a ride this had been for Whitworth's baseball team. The year before, in 1959, this same group had qualified for the national tournament and been invited to participate as Evergreen Conference Champions. Unfortunately, Whitworth's athletic budget rarely stretched far enough to include the cost of post-season travel, and there was no money to fund a trip to the national championship. When Whitworth had to decline the invitation, Western Washington College was afforded the opportunity to go in their stead. The disappointment was bitterly felt by everyone, none more so than my father. Most of the players were underclassmen, many of whom were lettering in other sports, a typical situation for small-college athletes. Coach Merkel had delivered the bad news to his team and guaranteed, on the spot, that if each one of them came back to play the next year, they would once again be invited to participate in the NAIA national tournament. And this time, he promised that they would go to the tournament if he had to mortgage his house to do so. The team believed him and they all returned, including Ray Washburn, their fire-balling right hander; Tom Ingram, another ace right-hander; and Norm Harding, a fiercely talented shortstop. Whether my mother ever knew about the promise her husband made that day is unclear, but likely she would have stood beside him and joined in his somewhat rash pronouncement.

Eighteen Whitworth baseball players made the trip to Sioux City,

Iowa, in June 1960. As Evergreen Conference Champions, the Pirates carried the banner for Area 1 (including the states of Washington, Oregon, Idaho, California, Nevada, Montana, and Wyoming) in the Fourth Annual NAIA Baseball "World Series." Still in its infancy, the tournament was nevertheless beginning to attract interest across the country not only from participating colleges but also from Major League Baseball scouts.

In all, eight teams were invited to participate in the double elimination tournament. It was the first time the tournament was held outside the state of Texas, and this year Morningside College in Sioux City served as the host school with all games being played at Soos Park, a minor league ball field not far from campus. Accommodations were rudimentary; teams stayed in the dormitories at Morningside and ate meals in the campus dining hall. Because the facilities at Soos Park were inadequate for all eight teams to use, players were forced to dress and shower in the dorms before and after games.

Soos Park was the home of the Sioux City Soos, a minor league affiliate of the New York Giants. In 1959 the farm club had been downgraded from Class A (Western League) to Class B (Illinois-Indiana-Iowa League). Originally constructed in 1947, the stadium was designed to seat approximately 5,000 spectators, but by 1960, attendance was waning and it was falling into disrepair.

The accommodations hardly mattered to the Whitworth ballplayers. They were just happy to be there.

At the end of the regular season, Pirate team members had eagerly awaited word as to which team would be selected to represent Area 1 in the tournament. Sophomore pitcher Tom Ingram refused to go to class until he heard one way or another, camping outside of Coach Merkel's office on the day the invitations were handed out.

The "official" announcement was made during chapel. A telegram had arrived from Bob Livingston, the Area 1 chairman, directed to Paul Merkel, in his position as director of athletics:

"Whitworth Is Area 1 Rep. Oregon College of Education is alternate. Send complete Publicity immediately to A. W. Buckingham Morningside College Sioux City, Iowa. Sincere personal congratulations."

Coach Merkel beamed as he made the announcement and called a special team meeting immediately afterwards. He explained to the team that he didn't know how they were going to get there, but he had accepted the invitation on Whitworth's behalf and practice started that afternoon.

It was May 22, 1960, and the end of the school year not only for Whitworth but also for other colleges in the area. As a result, no collegiate teams were available for practice games before the tournament started. Ever resourceful, my father managed to scout out a couple of intramural squads at Fairchild Air Force Base who agreed to scrimmage with the tournament-bound Pirates. They were little match for Whitworth, all three games providing lopsided wins for the Pirates. But it was good practice and provided the necessary playing time to keep team members game ready. It also afforded senior captain Jim Glennon the unexpected opportunity to add a statistic to his baseball career that had to that point eluded him: a recorded stolen base.

For all his skill at catcher, Jim was ponderously slow on the bases. He had never stolen a base, nor had he even attempted the feat, knowing, first of all, that Coach Merkel would neither condone nor support wasting a man on base for an attempt that was doomed to failure. A man on base meant the possibility of a run, and you didn't sacrifice a potential run on a whim, or in this case, on the highly unlikely premise that Jim could beat out a throw to second. Norm Harding used to joke that you couldn't tell if Jim was moving unless you looked behind him. However, during one of the games against Fairchild, Jim found himself on first base with an opposing catcher he knew was suffering from bursitis. The catcher's pain made him barely able to throw the ball back to the pitcher. Jim stepped off first base and caught the attention of Coach Merkel, who was standing in the third base coach's box. Jim hopefully flashed the steal sign, addressed more as a question than a statement. Now my father was not without a sense of humor, and this game did not pack the same importance of a conference game, but I can imagine the look that was exchanged with his stalwart catcher, who was now crouched a little off first base. To his credit, Dad didn't crack a smile; he just turned away with a shrug, leaving the decision to stay or run up to Jim. Knowing that was as much of a blessing as he was going to get, Jim took off running with the next pitch. He got his stolen base, but just barely. He also got a fair amount of good-natured teasing from teammates and coaches after the game.

As soon as the invitation to play was received and accepted, coaches, ballplayers, and administrators got to work trying to piece together travel money to get the team to the tournament. Girlfriends canvassed the dorms collecting donations from students, a dollar at a time; local businesses were called and every service organization on campus was solicited for contributions. As was his custom, my dad kept meticulous records of the donations the team received for their trip: individual donations from friends and businesses ranged from as little as $2 to as much as $250. The Whitworth Student Body fund contributed $150 and the Whitworth Pirateers generously added $400 from their booster club. All contributions, no matter how large or how small, were welcomed.

In the end, just over $1,600 was raised for the weeklong trip to Sioux City. It wasn't a lot of money, but Coach Merkel was used to running the program on a shoestring. It would simply have to suffice to cover gas and hamburgers for their 2,500-mile trip to and from Sioux City. Coach Merkel secured a rental car from Avis. Pitcher Ray Washburn's sister lent them her car, while catcher Denny Rieger offered to drive his relatively new '56 Dodge and utility second baseman Jerry McCracken volunteered the use of his eye-catching convertible. Those who drove their own cars were each allotted a $200 stipend for the cost of gas and wear and tear on their vehicles. With gas at 25 cents a gallon, the stipend was considered a generous one.

Four cars and sixteen ballplayers, including Coach Merkel and Assistant Coach Ken Wittenburg, left campus at 6:20 a.m. on Friday morning, June 3, 1960. My mother had uncharacteristically rousted my sisters and me out of bed early in order to accompany our father to the team's rendezvous point on campus. We watched through eyes still heavy with disrupted sleep as the ballplayers were divided between the four waiting cars, their gear safely stowed in the trunks. It was the only time I can remember actually being there to see them off. And yet we still had no idea that this trip was any different from any of the others that took our father and his baseball team on the road. At the ages of ten, eight, and six, we did not attend many games and so it was difficult for Coach Merkel's three young daughters to feel connected to his work, either on or off the field. All we knew was that during baseball season, Dad was seldom home. In our bubble of oblivion, exactly where he went and what he did eluded us. However, even seen from a distance, the young men with whom my father spent the greatest percentage of his time conjured within each of us a degree of awe and reverence normally reserved for TV stars or super heroes. They were The Baseball Team. Nothing further was required to fit iconic status in our eyes. Occasionally my father would bring one of his student athletes home for dinner, particularly during Thanksgiving or Easter, when some of the students remained on campus rather than make the long, often costly trip home. At those momentous times, our eyes wide with wonder, we would shyly approach the dining room table, our best manners in place. We were especially careful not to giggle or "carry on" in a manner that might embarrass the coach and bring his disfavor on us. For my sisters and me, those dinners created a tangible connection with our father's baseball world.

Of course, we weren't the only ones present to see the team off that morning. Several professors and administrators, along with wives, girlfriends and other well-wishers comprised the small group gathered with us to see the baseball team off on their journey. As they closed their eyes in silent supplication, Dr. David Dilworth, a pastor and professor of religion, offered up a fervent prayer that those four vehicles would withstand the trip and deliver the team safely to their destination. Recollections of previous road trips this team had taken were perhaps instrumental in eliciting this prayerful sendoff. The baseball budget didn't even allow for bus travel back and forth across the state and so, for each trip, team members pooled their resources and their various vehicles and drove. As far as anyone could remember, there was never a time when one of the cars didn't break down or suffer a flat tire on one of those trips.

It was admittedly a tight squeeze, fitting fourteen young men, two coaches, and all their equipment into the four compact cars, but fortunately the two remaining ballplayers were graduating seniors and despite some heavy lobbying, college officials insisted that they attend commencement exercises being held the Sunday before the tournament was set to start. Thus, senior catcher and team captain Jim Glennon and senior outfielder Ron Lince flew into Sioux City on Monday morning, arriving almost a full day behind the rest of the team.

4:
Road Trip

The trip to Sioux City was an arduous one, covering over 1,200 miles of two-lane highways in largely unfamiliar territory. Due to road construction, they were regularly rerouted onto detours, which made it even more imperative that the cars travel together as closely as possible. As was his custom, Coach Merkel situated himself in the lead car. The trailing car was Jerry McCracken's, with the other two cars sandwiched in between.

Traveling caravan fashion worked relatively well thanks to my father's careful planning and attention to detail. Each time they started up, he would call everyone together and schedule a predetermined meet-up point so they could stretch their legs and regroup. The routine proved its worth on their very first day of travel. The athletes riding in Jerry McCracken's convertible, including pitcher Tom Ingram and outfielder Lee Archer, decided to make an unscheduled stop somewhere outside of Billings, Montana, to change drivers and grab a quick bathroom break. It wasn't a long stop, but when they resumed driving they found themselves at a fork in the road with no indication as to which direction the lead vehicles had taken. After some discussion, they elected to go straight ahead, not realizing that Coach Merkel had taken another route to avoid some looming road construction up ahead. There being no way to communicate with the rest of their teammates, Jerry's group lagged well behind the others. They did not catch up with them until their next scheduled stop in Broadus, Montana.

Coach Merkel was none too happy that Jerry's vehicle had fallen so far behind the rest of the group. From personal experience, I know that my Dad did not appreciate what might be considered a foolish stunt or serious lapse in judgment. But even more than that was his personal sense of responsibility for the safety and well being of his players. I can imagine him pacing and fretting, his hand nervously pulling at his chin, as he waited anxiously for the wayward car to arrive. Dad was a handsome man, dark hair and rugged good looks accentuated with a Roman nose, paying homage to his Italian roots. Matched with my mother's blond beauty, they made a striking couple. When he laughed and smiled he could charm the socks off any woman, young or old, including his adoring daughters. To me, he was John Wayne. And Mom was Grace Kelly. But when he was upset, his countenance took on a much sterner, darkly ominous look. I pitied anyone who unleashed that look from my Dad, no matter who they were and no matter what the circumstances.

In this instance, Dad's displeasure had a lasting effect on the stragglers. From that time forward, catcher Denny Rieger took over as driver of the lead car and Coach Merkel's car brought up the rear. Jerry's car, now firmly nestled in the middle, never strayed from the caravan again. Coach would review the projected route with Denny each time they started out, but he also scheduled more frequent check-in stops along the way. One thing was made clear, no one was to pass the lead car for fear of losing their evening meal privileges. Nothing more needed to be said.

Hardly more than a village in 1960, Broadus, Montana, was situated along the Powder River just below the Little Bighorn Mountains. This was cattle and oil country. Little else in the way of commerce existed in that part of Montana. Sporting a restaurant or two, one motel, and a couple of bars, it occupied space in the midst of several Native American reservations, about halfway between Spokane and Sioux City. Knowing my father's penchant for numbers and statistics, I have no trouble believing that he chose Broadus as their stopping point precisely for that reason, because it was about as close to halfway between Spokane and Sioux City as he was going to find.

Numbers were as much a part of my father's life as was baseball. Manipulating numbers came so easily to him that he seldom used a calculator when working up the stats of a game or a season. A favorite exercise for him was to challenge his mental capacity against a calculator. I remember Mom's stories of him adding, multiplying or dividing six- and seven-digit numbers in his head while a student would quickly do the same function on a calculator. Nine times out of ten Dad would come up with the correct answer before the challenger had finished entering the last of the numbers into the calculator. And he was never wrong. So when he chose Broadus, Montana, as the halfway point, I have little doubt that that is exactly what it was.

Whitworth College senior photograph of Irene Pruter Merkel *circa* 1947. *Reprinted courtesy of Whitworth University Archives.*

The Pirate baseball team spent their first night on the road at the C–J (C bar J) Motel. Understandably, the C–J Motel, named after the owner's horse and cattle brand, was not a four-star establishment, nor was it particularly large, but it was clean and cheap and the choice of accommodations in Broadus was limited. Enough rooms were reserved to accommodate two to three players in each room. Coach Merkel and his assistant coach, Ken Wittenburg, occupied the one available room that boasted two twin beds. The rest of the rooms afforded only a single double bed, so inevitably someone had to sleep on the floor. It was a tossup as to which was preferable, sharing the bed with a teammate or sleeping on the floor.

At exactly 7:30 the next morning the team was on the road again. Dad had calculated that by leaving at 7:30 they could expect to roll into Sioux City at about 11:00 that night, Saturday, June 4. Teams were expected to check in on Sunday, prior to the kickoff banquet that evening, and the games started Monday.

Although Coach Merkel was a stickler for driving the speed limit at all times, 50 to 60 miles an hour, depending on road conditions and detours, did not get them very far, very fast. During the season, team members would find any excuse possible to relieve their coach of his driving responsibilities, always hoping that once he became a passenger he would fall asleep. And when he did, well, whoever was driving that lead car would gradually speed up to 70 or 75 mph. Drivers in the other cars remained alert for this strategy to play out. Miraculously, no car was ever left behind even at the greater speeds. If he ever knew about this clandestine pact, Coach never said, although he did mumble to himself a time or two that he hadn't expected to "make it quite this far so quickly."

During the trip, check-in points were determined for several purposes: to eat, to take bathroom breaks, and sometimes just to get out of the cars and loosen up. At those times they would don their gloves and toss balls back and forth, shag ground balls and run around enough to work the kinks out of their muscles. It was fun. Sometimes they would take the opportunity, after stopping for a meal, to "practice" in the restaurant parking lot. On one such occasion their waitress was a particularly colorful woman, sporting several tattoos and flirting shamelessly with the ballplayers and their coach. In a fit of bravado the team made it known that they were on their way to Sioux City to win the NAIA baseball tournament. Whether she believed them or not, she challenged them to stop on their way home and show her the trophy. And they promised they would.

The route out of Rapid City, South Dakota, proved to be long and flat, through scrublands that were uninspiring and brown. First baseman Jerry Breymeyer described it as "the kind of place only Mother Nature could love." At a particularly remote rest stop in the middle of the Badlands, the parched earth stretched out before them, unencumbered with trees or other restrictive vegetation. The uninterrupted expanse provided a perfect location for batting practice and launching high fly balls. Always eager to leave the cramped confines of their cars, the Pirate ballplayers grabbed their equipment for a little hitting and fielding practice. Each team member carried their own personal gloves and bats. Coach Merkel supplied the balls and the uniforms.

The area was flat all right, but it was also tableland that sat atop a rather spectacular canyon, typical for this area of the country. The canyon rim, looming several hundred yards east of their parked cars, presented an enticing invitation to try their hands at hitting balls hard enough and far enough to disappear over the edge of the canyon, as well as throwing balls as far as they could with the same purpose. Joyously, carelessly, they watched ball after ball disappear over the canyon rim, concerned only with testing their individual prowess against the inviting expanse of space. It was great fun while the balls lasted, but Coach Merkel was not amused. They lost most of the balls he had brought with them. He reminded the thirteen mostly contrite ballplayers that

Paul J. Merkel in the dugout at Spokane Indians Ball
Park, summer 1970. *Photographer unknown.*

replacement balls would have to be paid for out of their scant travel funds. As a result of their "fun," a trip to a sporting goods store would have to be scheduled when they arrived in Sioux City so he could replenish their supply. Money was tight, and this was an unexpected expense the team could ill afford.

My dad would have scowled as he issued his reprimand, but maybe, just maybe, he would have smiled inwardly. His own college days were not that far behind him. He had been a serious student, all the while lettering in three sports and maintaining an active role in campus leadership. But he was not without a mischievous side. One stunt in particular was notable, a stunt he and his cohorts might have gotten away with had a guilty conscience and innate sense of responsibility not interfered.

In 1942, plans were actualized for the construction of a brand new gymnasium on campus. Excavation of the site had proven to be a challenge; bulldozers unearthing rocks and boulders the size of small cars. One night, as the construction site lay dormant of activity, Paul Merkel, then a sophomore, and a couple of his friends went to work on one of the larger boulders, skillfully etching replica petroglyph figures onto one side of the stone face with nothing more than pocket knives. Satisfied with their work, they rolled some smaller rocks up against the masterpiece of "ancient art" to give the new rock scars a more scuffed and weathered look. Then they returned to their dorm to wait.

The practical jokers did not have long to wait. Construction workers noticed the petroglyphs almost immediately and called in school officials, who in turn notified the state historic society and a museum curator to come and have a look. And look they did. And taken in they were. So realistic did the etchings appear that the "find" was reported to the Smithsonian and representatives agreed to come out to tiny Whitworth College to investigate the historic significance of the petroglyphs, the first ever found in the Spokane area. It was about that time that the pranksters stepped forward, admitting their deed and throwing their student careers on the mercy of Whitworth administrators. Whatever punishment was meted out was never revealed by my father. Suffice it to say, he remained in school.

5:

On Deck

The team arrived in Sioux City, Iowa, late Saturday night, greeted by an uncustomary profusion of smells from the surrounding stockyards and packing houses, made even more pungent by the hot, sultry humidity that hung in the air. They were assured by local residents they met that night that the wind usually blew in the opposite direction from the Morningside College campus and the baseball park so they shouldn't be bothered by the smell too much during the games. The offhand reassurance was delivered with a knowing smile and received with a somewhat skeptical nod of thanks.

Sioux City boasted a unique blend of urban and rural living. With a population of less than 80,000, spread over an area of 56 square miles, Sioux City is located very near the center of the North American continent, sitting at the confluence of three rivers: the Missouri, the Floyd, and the Big Sioux. Commerce consisted mainly of farming, ranching, and packing houses.

After spending Saturday night in a nearby hotel, Coach Paul Merkel and his Whitworth Pirate baseball squad checked in with tournament headquarters at 1:00 p.m. on Sunday afternoon, June 5. The opening banquet did not start until six that evening, so they took advantage of the extra time to get in a short workout before returning to the dormitory to dress for dinner. The exertion provided some much-needed relaxation after the long hours spent in their cars and allowed some of their pent-up energy to dissipate before the banquet.

Traveling such a great distance within the confined space of their cars, with little to do but idly talk or nap when not driving or serving as navigator, had been mind numbingly tedious. Whenever tedium overtook them, the more playful and daring of the bunch would find ways to stay amused. Being little more than kids themselves, their amusement was at times ill advised if not outright dangerous, like throwing things out the car windows as they motored down the highway. Banana peels and sometimes whole ripe bananas were favorite missiles, as were pint-sized milk cartons still full of milk. The athletes had discovered quite by accident that a ripe banana would stick to the side of a car, and after being wind whipped and cooked by the sun, it would harden until it was nearly impossible to scrape off. But the milk cartons were a favorite. What a mess that made, much to the delight of the missile launchers. I have to believe that this activity was practiced primarily when their coach was either asleep or in the lead car, well out in front of the others. Admittedly, food and drink missiles were a poor substitute for being able to take batting practice, shag fly balls or run the bases.

Whitworth's normal warm-up routine before a game was to take batting practice, do a little infield work, and loosen their arms. Generally these practices were considered fun, especially when compared to their early pre-season workouts. Coach Merkel believed that a good player required good physical conditioning. Pre-season workouts were purposely strenuous. For the first two weeks of practice they concentrated on circuit training and didn't even pick up a bat or a ball. Because the only indoor athletic facility in those days was drafty old Graves Gymnasium, where basketball games were played and gym classes were held, Coach Merkel would work with the pitchers and catchers first. The remainder of the team members would run up and down the gym stairs or stand in the roughly taped-out "batter's box" and watch pitches fly by. Coach's attention would then turn towards the infielders. He would hit balls to them, one after another in quick succession, while the rest of the team ran the stairs. He made these early practices as strenuous as possible so that those who were less committed and not so determined would quit, thereby cutting themselves before Coach had to cut anyone, a notion he never did care for.

Once the season started, practices settled into a congenial routine. Everyone practiced together. Even those that were on the "practice team" hit against the starting pitchers and rotated fielding practice with the starting infielders. Coach Merkel emphasized fundamentals without spending a lot of time with any one individual at his position. Ever mindful that baseball is a game of constantly changing variables, he spent considerable time on game situations. The number of men on base, which base has runners aboard, how many outs there are, the inning and the score, all determine what a player does with the ball if it comes his way, whether he is a pitcher, catcher or fielder. So Coach would hit fungoes to the infielders, calling out various game situations. Then, if someone made a poor decision, Coach would correct them and try again with an entirely different set of circumstances. He believed in being proficient in the basics, his philosophy being that if you did the small things well, the results would take care of themselves. Pitchers were instructed to throw strikes and leave it to those behind them to field the balls and make the outs.

Utility infielder Don Cox was on the practice team for two years before he started getting any playing time. Twice during that two-year span, Don, a newcomer to the sport of baseball, skipped practice, believing it wouldn't matter if he was there or not, since he wasn't a starter. But both times Coach Merkel made it a point to talk to him about missing practice. It made Don feel like a valued member of the team and reinforced the importance of attending all practices.

Don graduated from Spokane's North Central High School and had come to Whitworth expecting to play football. However, during his first fall practice, it became apparent that Don's short stature and lack of significant bulk made it severely unlikely he would ever play football. My dad was the backfield coach that year, and as was his habit he noted Don's determination and "don't quit" attitude, despite the odds against him. That indomitable spirit was always present, and that was just the kind of player my father loved to recruit for his baseball team. Besides, it was a shame to waste that kind of commitment. When he finally approached Don about playing baseball, Don's initial reluctance was understandable. He hadn't played baseball in high school, and he was not so sure about changing over now that he was in college. But Coach Merkel kept at him, knowing that football was probably a dead end and believing they could teach him the mechanics and fundamentals of baseball. It would be up to Don to bring his passion to a different game. In the end Don agreed to give it a try. For his efforts, he gradually worked his way to the starting team where he shared second base honors with Bill Trenbeath and Jerry McCracken.

6:
Held Up

Twenty minutes later and rain was still falling, although there was a fantasy of hope that it had lessened in intensity. Whitworth had taken an early lead (a strategy Coach Merkel cultivated throughout the season) and their ace, Ray Washburn, was on the rubber, doggedly holding Georgia Southern scoreless through three innings. How long he could keep his arm warm, the muscles loose enough to continue pitching was a question on everyone's mind as they milled around the dugout, saying little. Ray was a competitor; 6'1" and 200 lbs., a strong right-handed pitcher with a blazing fastball. During the tournament he had also proven adept at mixing in sharp curve balls and sliders, and every once in a while a killer breaking ball. The ability to effectively mix up his pitches caught the eye of more than one Major League scout. In all, 15 of the 16 Major League teams had scouts in attendance at various times throughout the tournament.

As the teams waited, gasoline was once again spread along the infield base paths and ignited, burning off as much of the standing water as possible. The stench was overpowering, but most of the spectators who were in attendance had moved to warmer, drier locales. Only a few remained, including Bill Trenbeath's parents, who had driven down from North Dakota to see their son play in the national tournament.

***

Ray Washburn on the mound at NAIA Baseball Tournament, June 1960. *Photo credited to Don Murphy, photographer, Sioux City, Iowa.*

Bill Trenbeath was one of three players who rotated in at second base. He had come to Whitworth the year before as a transfer student from the University of North Dakota where he had been a chemical engineering major. He later described the move as the smartest one he ever made. Bill's familiarity with the roads between Spokane and South Dakota proved especially beneficial to the uninitiated travelers and made him a useful resource when determining the best route to take on the way to Sioux City and the logical choice to drive much of the way.

***

The wait was unnerving. It was the championship game. Tomorrow they would be driving home. Georgia Southern represented Area 7 (Georgia, Florida, North and South Carolina, Tennessee and West Virginia) and came into the tournament with a 17–9–1 regular season record, boasting wins at Kentucky, South Carolina and Florida State. Whitworth's record was, by comparison, unimpressive at 13–7. In a pre-game interview Coach Merkel acknowledged that Georgia Southern had two terrific pitchers in Travis Rivers and Ray Mims and that they expected to see Mims on the mound that afternoon. He also admitted that, despite a day of rest, Whitworth was still considered the underdog. There was a reason for that.

7:
Rubber Match

Since the start of the tournament, Whitworth's most significant games had been played against Georgia Southern. In fact, the championship game was the third time these two squads had squared off. Each team had managed a win. Their first meeting came during the second day of the tournament and saw Whitworth come out with a 1–0 win in a pitchers' duel that wasn't decided until the ninth inning. Tom Ingram, an ace right-hander in his own right, proved unrelenting, striking out twelve and holding Georgia Southern's highly touted offense to just three hits.

Tom was a sophomore, heralding from Yakima, Washington. Built stockier and closer to the ground than Ray Washburn, Tom was nevertheless a standout pitcher in high school and had received scholarship offers from a couple of bigger universities, including the University of Washington. However, Tom had heard stories about the unwieldy class sizes and the anonymity facing students at UW, and he wasn't sure that he wanted to get lost in the crowd of such a large state university. He knew Jim and Jerry Breymeyer, both of whom attended Whitworth and were involved in the football and baseball programs there. Jerry's account of his experiences both at the college and playing ball for Coach Merkel convinced Tom that he was better suited to a small college environment. With Coach Merkel's help in securing a scholarship, Tom arrived at Whitworth in 1959 and easily settled into the second starter role behind Washburn. But being the second starter meant that, unlike Ray, Tom did not play another position on the team. He had to be available to pitch the second game of their doubleheaders, and Coach didn't want him playing in the first game and getting injured or tired out. He needed to be ready to pitch in the night cap. Because he didn't play other positions, the job of keeping up the scorebook generally fell to him. He already kept stats for both the football and basketball teams and managing the scorebook when he wasn't pitching was a logical progression.In the fourth inning of that first meeting, Georgia Southern was in their best position to get on the scoreboard, with two outs and a runner on third. Coach Merkel made an uncustomary trip to the mound to talk with Ingram and his catcher, Jim Glennon. In general Coach made it a point to let his pitcher and catcher choose their pitches and manage the game the way they saw fit, seldom coming to the mound to confer on any one batter. This was an exception. A passed ball had advanced the runner, and he wanted to give his pitcher and catcher a chance to shake it off.

Taking the ball from his catcher, I can almost see Dad massaging it between his rough hands, turning it over and over, as if the friction of hands on horsehide could transmit his intention and desire into the very fabric of the ball. He didn't need to say much as he looked Tom squarely in the eyes. I had been the recipient of that same look, even at the age of ten: intent, but not disapproving. It was meant to bring focus back to the task at hand and to elicit the very best out of the person on whom that look was directed. Still massaging the ball, he simply stated, "You know what to do." Then he dropped the ball into Tom's glove, and with a quick pat on his pitcher's back pocket and a glance towards the infield, Coach Merkel strode back to the dugout.

The brief hiatus proved beneficial for the entire team, allowing everyone to relieve their building tension before play resumed. Ingram, who was not easily rattled, struck out the next Georgia Southern batter with four well-placed pitches and eliminated the only scoring threat Georgia Southern was to have in that game. The Pirates' victory, however, was ultimately decided on a play that surprised everyone, including the ballplayers themselves.

Tom Ingram in action at NAIA Baseball Tournament, June 1960.
Photo credited to Don Murphy, photographer, Sioux City, Iowa.

In the bottom of the ninth, center fielder Lee Archer walked. It was getting late. The game had started at 8:30 p.m. Fatigue was setting in. Tracy Rivers, Georgia Southern's lanky ace pitcher, tried to pick Lee off first base but his throw was wild, bouncing into the Whitworth dugout. Lee scampered to third base, advancing an extra base according to Soos Park Ground rules that dictated "any ball from the field of play that goes into a dugout is declared dead and entitles the runner to advance one base."

Coach Merkel was at his customary place in the third base coach's box. Norm Harding was up. Norm, who had also caught the eye of several Major League scouts during the tournament, was Whitworth's shortstop. Lee noticed Coach Merkel giving signals fast and furiously. That, in and of itself, was highly unusual since he was generally slow and precise in his movements, even if the signals didn't mean anything. Signals were stolen by opposing teams all the time, so most of the shrugs, gestures, and hand movements Coach Merkel went through were meant as a ruse more than anything. However, amongst all the gesturing, Coach moved his hand up to stroke his chin. Just once. Skin on skin. It was the signal that the next sign really meant something. Lee was instantly alert. Coach was deliberately walking away from home plate with his hands in his back pockets, pulling up his pants. Was that the sign for a squeeze bunt?

Doubt crept in. Coach hadn't used that sign all year. But the pitcher was going into his windup and Lee had no time to ponder the situation. He had to act. With a fleeting "Oh, crap!" muttered under his breath, Lee broke for home plate as soon as the ball left the pitcher's hand. He didn't dare look at Coach on the way by, in case he had guessed wrong. He was just hitting his stride as Norm laid down the perfect bunt. If there was any doubt about Lee's speed on the bases, it was erased that night. Even Lou Brock, the highly regarded outfielder for Southern University, would have been hard pressed to win that race from third base to home plate. Lou was fast and had set numerous school and conference records for stolen bases during his college career, attracting his own fair share of interest among Major League scouts. His mere presence on base elicited a certain degree of angst with opposing pitchers. But that night it was Lee Archer racing home and scoring what would be the winning run. The team erupted onto the field. Other than Lee, only one other player had gotten as far as third base during the entire game, and Tom Ingram had fired past twelve Georgia Southern batters, adding to the burgeoning strikeout totals of Whitworth's two top pitchers.

The second game against Georgia Southern was played late Thursday night and didn't go as well for Whitworth. Even their on-field warm-ups had proven embarrassing as balls were over-thrown and grounders slipped heedlessly through outstretched gloves. Admittedly, the weather was nasty. The field was slippery with rain and the heat and humidity were unrelenting. Infielders would throw balls that dropped like lead weights well before their intended targets, making it even more difficult to throw runners out on base. Even Farrell Romig, a reliable outfielder in most situations, lost track of a couple of fly balls as rain coated his glasses and obscured his vision. Three Whitworth pitchers attempted to stop the onslaught of runs, including starter Tom Ingram, who was facing Georgia Southern for the second time. By the seventh inning the score was 12–1 in favor of the Eagles. Mercifully, tournament rules mandated that if any team was ahead by 10 runs at the end of seven innings, the game would be called. When the game ended, Ray Washburn's home run (Ray was playing right field that night) accounted for Whitworth's lone score.

Tom took the loss as a bitter disappointment, in himself more than anything. With the kind of knowledge that comes only from family, the telegram the team got from the Ingrams the next day helped assuage their son's dismay:

```
June 11, 1960 - 8:00 a.m.
To: Whitworth Team
From: The Ingrams

"We're not mad - win or lose you can come
home! Make it a good game. Good luck."
```

Telegrams were the primary method of communication between Whitworth and their supporters back home. The Ingrams had been faithful cheer leaders and correspondents, sending telegrams nearly every day. Coach Ross Cutter had leant his support of the team he swore only made it to the tournament because of his stellar abilities as relief coach while my dad was ill:

```
June 9, 1960 - 11:00 a.m.
To: Whitworth Team
From: The Frat House - 7515 Laurelhurst
(Cutter residence)

"Keep up the great work. The whole town is
jumping. We're all with you."
```

And the president of the college sent this:

```
June 9, 1960 - Noon
To: Whitworth Team
From: President Warren, faculty and
staff

"Congratulations on your victories. We're
all rooting for you in tonight's game. Go
get 'um."
```

With money as scarce as it was, my mother stalwartly waited to send our family's congratulations until Whitworth's finish was solidified.

Georgia Southern's win on Thursday forced a three-way tie for the title game. Immediately following the game, a coin flip was used to determine which two teams would collide in the "loser-out" game and which team would have the bye. Coach Merkel, on behalf of the Whitworth squad, called the coin toss correctly, advancing Whitworth automatically into the championship contest that was scheduled to start at 2:00 p.m. on Saturday. The play-in game was scheduled for Friday night. Georgia Southern would face Southern University, the defending national champion. After four games in as many days, the bye gave Whitworth's star hurlers, Ray Washburn and Tom Ingram, a chance to get some much-needed rest. Relief pitching had been ineffectual on Thursday, and the championship game was going to depend on the arm strength of their starting pitchers.

Southern University came into the 1960 tournament as the defending champion and odds on favorite. Southern was an all-black university from Baton Rouge, Louisiana. Although baseball, and particularly college baseball, had been integrated for many years, even before Jackie Robinson broke the color-barrier in the majors, there were still relatively few black baseball players in 1960, and racial tensions were not unheard of on the baseball field. It was debatable whether those tensions were generated amongst the players themselves or simply carried over from intolerant administrators and boosters. It was no secret that one team had been told by a school administrator that if they let Southern beat them, they would have to find their way back to Texas through Mexico. Perhaps it was no accident, then, that NAIA officials had housed Southern on an adjacent floor and in the same dormitory with Whitworth, a Christian college without geographical or historical animosity or prejudice against an all-black team.

The Southern Jaguars boasted two noteworthy players, including pitcher Charlie Gray, who had allowed only three earned runs over forty-eight regular season innings, a staggering feat. The other player attracting a lot of attention was L. C. (Lou) Brock, their speedy base-stealing right fielder. Southern represented Area 5 (Arkansas, Louisiana, Mississippi, Alabama, and Kentucky.) Southern's team batting average was an intimidating .335, and their team pitching ERA was a collective 2.10. With a regular season record of 21–3, it was no wonder that this team was considered the favorite to win a second title. But Georgia Southern had been up to the challenge and walked away with a 3–1 win Friday night, which forced the third game rubber match with Whitworth for the championship.

8:
Bringing The Heat

Finally, after a thirty-two-minute hiatus in the biggest game of their lives, it looked as though the rain was relenting. The sky was still dark and menacing, and a damp drizzle continued to fall, but the umpires were conferring on the field. Because Whitworth is a Christian college and because NAIA policy disapproved of Sunday competitions, calling the game on account of rain and mud would have created a host of problems. The expense of holding the teams over until Monday was prohibitive. In addition, any teams and supporters remaining at the tournament were scheduled to leave Saturday night and Sunday morning, so playing the championship game on Monday afternoon, would have guaranteed a meager crowd at best. Officials even discussed the prospects of ending the tournament with cochampions. But the players and coaches from both squads expressed a desire to play the game if at all possible. So the decision was made. Both teams and the officials were in agreement. For Whitworth, this game, these conditions, were not so much different than what they had grown accustomed to during their regular season. They knew how to dress for this weather and they knew how to play in it.

As expected, Ray Washburn, Whitworth's flame-throwing right-hander, had been tapped to start the championship game. After three days, he was well rested and ready to go. At that point in the tournament, Ray had pitched sixteen total innings. He held an impressive 0.00

ERA, with 34 strikeouts and only 5 base-on-balls. Opposing teams had managed to get a meager 5 hits, all singles, off of him.

***

Throughout the regular season Ray relied heavily on his fastball to overpower opposing batters. Not surprisingly, he was called upon to pitch the Pirates' first tournament game against the host school, Morningside College, whose regular season record was a respectable 15 wins with only 4 losses. Affiliated with the United Methodist Church, Morningside was founded in 1894, and like Whitworth, was a four-year Christian-oriented college.

The Whitworth vs. Morningside game was the night cap for the first round, not starting until 8:30 p.m. on Monday night. It was customary for the host school to play the last game of the day and to be pitted against the lowest seeded team in the tournament, the theory being that the longer the host team was in the tournament, the more fans and local residents would attend the games. That custom was no secret to anyone. And Whitworth ballplayers were still smarting after an unintended slight they suffered during the official kickoff banquet the night before.

That Sunday, after attending 8:00 a.m. services at the First Presbyterian Church and signing in with tournament officials, Coach Merkel and the team headed to their designated practice field for a mini workout. The practice field was located in a city park not too far from campus. To describe the diamond and infield area as unkempt and rough was probably kind. Southern University was just finishing up their practice, and team members were running wind sprints in the outfield. They looked like a professional team to many of the Whitworth players: intimidating and fast. It was well known that Southern's team was composed of some speedy ballplayers, but the Jaguars also boasted the second fastest 440 relay team in the nation, second only to the incomparable USC. The next fastest foursome at Southern was comprised of four baseball players, all of whom were now running in the outfield. It was an impressive display, impressive enough that

Coach Merkel thought it might be a good idea for his players to run a few wind sprints as well. Running had always been a part of practice and warm-ups, but before that afternoon, never wind sprints. They all survived, but barely.

The team returned to Morningside College Men's Residence Hall to change for dinner. When they received their housing assignment, each player was given a pillow and one sheet. Clean towels were furnished daily. Denny Reiger, a sophomore catcher, had looked at the meager bedding with some concern. He hadn't expected a lot of amenities, but this seemed particularly spartan. Their first night in the dormitory proved how sufficient the bedding actually was. The night was so hot and humid that it was hard to breathe, and any bedding at all only enhanced the uncomfortable sweat soaking their backs.

This year, NAIA officials were launching their first annual baseball Hall of Fame banquet to lead-off the weeklong tournament in Sioux City. The eight teams competing in the tournament were invited as special guests. Unfamiliarity with the city contributed as much as anything to Whitworth being the last to arrive at the Sheraton-Martin Hotel, where the banquet was being held.

During dinner all of the teams were introduced. All, that is, except Whitworth. When Joe McDermott, a well-known New York Yankees scout and master of ceremonies that night, realized his error, he made his apologies and then referred to them as Washington College and then Washburn College before finally getting their name right. His remark at the end of that fiasco was that now Whitworth would probably go ahead and win the whole thing. It was meant as a joke. But perhaps this little slight solidified the resolve of each Whitworth team member to make these people remember their names by winning the championship both for themselves and for their coach. Whitworth was an unknown entity here in Sioux City. They had driven across four states in four ragtag cars while other teams arrived in shiny Greyhound buses or special charter buses with their team names emblazoned across the sides.

As anonymous as Whitworth's baseball team was among the other competitors in the tournament, my father was surprisingly well known among NAIA officials and many of the opposing coaches. Upon their arrival, the baseball team was amazed at the respect and admiration bestowed upon their coach. They hadn't realized how actively involved Coach Merkel was in the organization of the NAIA and the establishment of this baseball tournament, nor were they aware of the esteem with which he was held on a national level. There was more than a little desire to make their coach proud and win the whole thing.

That resolve probably carried through when Ray took the mound Monday night against Morningside. This was their first game, and they needed to win. The Maroon Chiefs' starting pitcher, Ken Stripling, had set a league record for wins that year and was batting .300. Their starting shortstop sported a .348 average. The Chiefs would not go down easily.

With his adrenaline amped to overflowing, Ray Washburn approached the mound fully intending to make a statement. He had successfully relied on his bread-and-butter fastball throughout the season and didn't intend to change that strategy now. He immediately went to work. Time and again he reared back, and then, like the spring-loaded ball launcher on a pin ball machine, he would thrust his body forward, releasing the ball like a missile. The velocity with which it crossed the plate left Morningside batters either frozen in their stance or swinging wildly as the ball smacked into Denny Rieger's waiting mitt. The effect must have been demoralizing for the hometown batters. For Denny, who was catching that game, as he always did when Ray was pitching, it was downright painful. Denny had felt his nerves tighten as the first batter approached the plate, but after a few pitches he and Ray settled into a familiar rhythm. They were well attuned to working together and they both wanted to win, if for no other reason than to prove that their team belonged in the tournament.

There was something a little more ferocious in Ray's fastballs that night. In the field, Ray's teammates stood ready, glad to a man that they were supporting the right-hander in the field and not facing him at the plate. Second baseman Jerry McCracken had firsthand knowledge of the speed and power of Ray's fastballs. Jerry was a sophomore from Denver, Colorado. Earlier in the season he had failed to get out of the way of one of those pitches during practice. A little too high and inside,

Ray Washburn in action at NAIA Baseball Tournament, June 1960.
Photo credited to Don Murphy, photographer, Sioux City, Iowa.

the ball had cold-cocked Jerry before he even saw it coming. The next thing Jerry knew, he was on the ground, opening his eyes to see the faces of concerned teammates looking down at him from all directions.

Jerry was another two-sport athlete, having transferred to Whitworth after Denver University discontinued its football program during Jerry's freshman year. With the demise of the program, Jerry lost his scholarship. Fortunately, Jerry knew Bill Knuckles, a coach with Whitworth's football program. Coach Knuckles encouraged Jerry to give Whitworth a chance, and the next year Jerry was on campus, ready to play ball. But Jerry's stature was small for a football player, barely 150 pounds at his heaviest, so he spent a lot of time on the bench. Never one to miss an opportunity or be deterred by a challenge, Jerry turned his sights to the baseball program and tried out for the team. He had always liked baseball and was hoping to find a sport that would allow him to spend less time riding the pine. With hard work, Jerry earned my father's attention and battled his way into a share of playing time at second base.

Even from the advantage of time, however, it was hard for him not to cringe inwardly with every fastball Ray was throwing past Morningside batters.

By the end of the game, Ray had pitched seven full innings, whiffing an astonishing seventeen batters and allowing no runs. Denny's hands were so sore from catching Ray's pitches that he had to wear a sponge in his glove as extra padding for the balance of the game. He was still using the extra padding during his next stint behind the plate.

Knowing that his arm was tiring and because they were comfortably ahead 7–0, Coach Merkel took Ray out of the Morningside game after seven innings and looked to freshman Spike Grosvenor to relieve. Morningside was able to close the gap to 7–4 in the eighth inning at Spike's expense and with the help of a couple of untimely infield errors. Although Whitworth still had a sizeable lead, Spike's wildness had gotten him in trouble and kept Denny Reiger off balance behind the plate.

Walter "Spike" Grosvenor was a sophomore from Spokane's West Valley High School. Spike had enlisted in the Army right after high school graduation and spent two years in Maryland before returning to Spokane to serve out the rest of his enlistment obligation in the reserves. At the time, West Valley boasted a large contingent of students attending Whitworth, many of whom Spike knew from either his church or Young Life. Whitworth seemed like the logical choice for pursuing a physical education degree while playing football and baseball.

Perhaps as a nod to his active military service, Spike sported a dark crew-cut and round, oversized black-rimmed glasses. His somewhat professorial look belied a mischievous character. He took chances, and sometimes it showed in his pitching. The side-winding movement of one curve ball left Denny flat on his face as he dived to halt its wayward trajectory, its startling swerve calling to mind the snakes the team had seen during their trip to Sioux City, in an exhibit housed at the infamous Wall Drug.

Like many travelers along the I-90 corridor, the caravan of ballplayers had started seeing the painted wooden signs advertising Wall Drug almost immediately after leaving Rapid City, South Dakota. And as have millions of travelers both before and after them, they too stopped at the roadside wonder. What quirk of fate managed to convince my father to make this stop has often baffled me since he was usually very focused on destination during road trips and not one to veer off course.

As a family, we did not take a lot of road trips or vacations, summers generally devoted to scouting and money being sparse at best. His job at Whitworth paid just enough to provide his three growing daughters with clothes, school supplies, and food, with little left over for frivolities like vacations. The trips we did take usually revolved around Dad's periodic speaking engagements at small community churches throughout the Inland Empire, these speaking engagements just one of several jobs he took to provide much-needed revenue during the three lean summer months when he did not receive a paycheck from the college. Dad joined a roster of Whitworth professors and administrators who stepped in to deliver Sunday sermons to churches in the small Washington communities of Colfax, Reardan, or Wellpinit when their own ministers were on vacation or if they were in between regular ministers. Whitworth's interim ministers could also find themselves assigned to Lapwai or Lewiston, Idaho. Although I don't remember a lot about the "messages" my father dutifully delivered to these rural congregations, I will never forget his go-to sermon: "Could This Be You?" He wove lessons about spiritual conviction around the fictional "Tator" family, the members of which he christened Dic Tator, Immi Tator, Aggi Tator, Hesi Tator, and Spec Tator. When I was twelve, Dad actually enlisted my burgeoning artistic talents to draw illustrative characterizations of the Tators, all bearing a striking resemblance to Mr. Potato Head figures in appropriate garb and attitude. What originally created within me a sense of self-important pride eventually became a source of some consternation as my father continued to use those crudely drawn illustrations in his Tator Family sermon, long after I was in high school.

Despite that fact that we didn't actually attend most of the church services at which Dad was the featured speaker—we usually remained in the car or were allowed to play at a near-by park while he addressed the congregation—my sisters and I and Mom and Dad would bundle into the old Rambler early on Sunday morning and make the drive to whichever community had requested a guest speaker. I recall wishing that we could stop at roadside attractions or places of interest, like the observation point at the top of the Lewiston grade. But stopping was not part of the plan for those Sunday drives. Destination trumped the journey every time. There was no stopping, no detours, no frills. He was singularly myopic in his determination to get where he was going.

And so, I still marvel at the serendipity that allowed the Whitworth Pirate baseball team to stop at a tourist trap like Wall Drug when they were on their way to a national tournament. Wall Drug had been in business since 1931 and at the time boasted not only free ice water but also a "serpentarium," an attraction that could only have been fully appreciated by a true snake lover but which did elicit at least a few nightmarish shivers, particularly for Spike. They stayed only long enough to briefly tour the shabby, cage-filled building and watch handlers feed a live white rat to one of the larger snakes before calling this excursion good and heading out again.

Since Spike just couldn't seem to get the last out of the inning, Coach Merkel decided to make a risky substitution, turning to Tom Ingram, who was slated to start their second game the next day.

"Can I use you?" he asked Tom.

There was no hesitation. "Shoot, yes!" he said, his customary bravado and self-confidence evident as he got ready to warm up. Actually this situation wasn't a lot different for Tom than during the regular season. His habit was to throw fifteen to twenty minutes of batting practice on the day before he was scheduled to start, as a kind of warm-up. Stepping in to pitch at the end of this crucial first game served the same purpose.

Tom pitched the last 1 and 1/3 innings against Morningside, allowing them no further hits or runs while Whitworth tacked on three insurance runs in the ninth.

9:
Leading Off

Despite the best efforts of the field crew, the infield had been muddy at the beginning of the championship game and the outfield was equally wet. Ray took the mound at the top of the first. He knew the team was depending on him, and he took his role seriously.

Georgia Southern sent their second baseman to lead off against Washburn. Ray let his shoulders drop, his back rounded as his arms hung loosely to his knees. Peering from under the brim of his cap, he fixed his laser focus on Denny's signal. Not surprisingly, Ray's first pitch was a well-positioned fastball for a called strike. The second pitch was hit just inside the first base line. First baseman Jerry Breymeyer deftly fielded the well-hit ball, tossing it to Washburn, covering first base for the easy out.

Next up for the Eagles was J. E. Rowe, their big center fielder, who took Ray's first pitch for strike one. On the next pitch Rowe connected with a sharp line drive to second baseman Bill Trenbeath who deftly threw the runner out at first. To this point, Ray had thrown only four pitches.

The top of the first was moving along quickly as third baseman and cocaptain Bill Mallard took his stance at the plate. Over their first two games Mallard had yet to get a hit off Whitworth pitchers, although the championship game was the first time Georgia Southern hitters had faced Washburn. But this time was no different as Mallard swung at

Ray's first pitch, hitting a little blooper directly into the waiting glove of Norm Harding. Three up and three down, with an economy of effort on the part of Ray and Whitworth's fielders.

Weather conditions being what they were, Whitworth had not been able to practice on either Thursday or Friday. While the rest was opportune for the pitchers, it may have been a detriment to the Pirate batters. Bill Trenbeath got the nod as lead-off hitter for Whitworth. Bill was a right-handed hitter, as were all of the Whitworth baseball players. There wasn't a lefty or a switch hitter among them. Whatever disadvantage this may have caused for other teams never materialized for Whitworth. In fact, they made up for it with multi-faceted players who could fill in at any position when needed. Of the non-starters, Coach Merkel could rely on at least two additional second basemen, Dale Roberts for relief pitching, and Abe Roberts as a skilled utility infielder, any one of them able to fill in wherever he was needed. That fact alone played a significant role in the strategy Coach Merkel used for each game. He had confidence that whatever the situation, he had players that could step in and handle any position, and he enjoyed watching them battle for their playing time.

Whether from nerves, impatience or lack of practice, Bill swung wildly at the first three pitches tossed by Ray Mims, Georgia Southern's starting pitcher, whiffing all three. Center fielder Lee Archer was up next, with .300 hitter Norm Harding on deck. Trenbeath's impatience was contagious. Mimicking Bill's at-bat, Lee went down swinging on the first three pitches thrown by Mims. Hitting in the third spot, Harding strode purposefully to the plate with the kind of confidence and intensity he usually displayed.

***

Norm Harding was a fierce competitor who had also attracted his fair share of attention from some of the Major League scouts in attendance at the tournament. Norm hailed from Spokane, attending little Rogers High School on the city's north side. Dad made a habit of attending area high school games when he got the opportunity, but most of his recruiting came from watching American Legion ball in the summers. I remember many summer evenings, hurrying through dinner, piling into the Rambler, and dashing off to one of the city parks to catch one, or maybe two, Legion games. My sisters and I would labor up the rickety wooden bleachers, clutching the hands of either Mom or Dad, to sit as close to the top as possible, the ground quite visible underneath our seats and foot rests. From that vantage point my Dad could easily watch all the players and it was here that he first noticed Norm, who was a pitcher at the time, and spoke to him about attending Whitworth. According to Norm, he would never have gotten to college without the influence and assistance of Coach Merkel.

At Rogers, Norm Harding lettered in both football and baseball. His intention had been to play both sports at WSU. However, the WSU football coach was recruiting Norm as a quarterback, and because spring practice was part of the Cougar football program, he would not release Norm to play baseball. Through the years, my Dad had learned to be an opportunist, but he may also have seen a little bit of himself in Norm, remembering too well the sting of disappointment he felt in not being able to play collegiate baseball himself. So he and the Whitworth football coach got together and talked to Norm about playing ball at Whitworth. The football team didn't need a quarterback, but they sure could use a halfback. Dad didn't need a pitcher, but he did need a shortstop. Norm was a natural athlete and a hard worker and he wanted to win. Those were qualities that Coach Merkel looked for in his ballplayers. Natural talent was great but heart was what he valued most. He could teach a player skills, but he couldn't teach character; that had to be there from the start. There were no baseball scholarships available at that time, but because Norm was such a versatile athlete, he was awarded a football scholarship and distinguished himself as a halfback as well as a shortstop during his college career.

The Whitworth baseball team was well aware and equally respectful of Norm's intensity. Like Ray Washburn, he was not shy about letting teammates know, in no uncertain terms, when they were not playing up to their capabilities or were slacking off. Like Ray, he also backed up his words with skillful, focused play on the field.

***

After taking a full count, Norm singled to right field. He positioned himself slightly off the bag at first, waiting for clean-up hitter Ray Washburn to send him home.

***

Not only was Ray their ace, but he was also one of Whitworth's most consistent hitters, with a tournament batting average of .294. Washburn took pride in his ability to contribute clutch hitting as well as solid pitching. In fact, he took it as a personal challenge to get a hit off every opposing pitcher he faced. In the game against Morningside he was embarrassed to strike out his first time at bat and the next time up hit into a fielder's choice. That was enough; at that point he vowed to hit one of Stripling's curve balls out of the park his next time up. In the fifth inning, after only one pitch, Ray did just that, hitting the ball so hard and so far that Bill Trenbeath joked that it was probably still in orbit somewhere, some fifty years later.

Ray grew up in Burbank, Washington, near Pasco. He came to Whitworth for his freshman year of college but circumstances dictated that he transfer back to Columbia Basin College, a junior college in the Tri Cities area for his sophomore year. Like many athletes in the 1960s, Ray successfully played two sports at the college level. While at Columbia Basin he played both baseball and basketball, leading their basketball team to the Northwest Junior College title. The baseball team went 25–3 the year Ray was at Columbia Basin. Ray returned to Whitworth for his junior and senior years.

Ray's competitive spirit matched Norm Harding's in intensity. It was not unusual for Ray to be at one end of the bench and Norm to be on the other with their teammates huddling in between the two. They were a formidable duo, and nobody wanted to be on the wrong end of their laser glares or their razor-sharp tongues.

***

With Norm on first and the count at 2 and 2, Ray could only manage a pop fly to the second baseman for the third out. The first inning was in the books.

Norm Harding in uniform *circa* 1962.
Photographer not identified.

10:
0-For

First up in the top of the second was Georgia Southern's left fielder. Hitting a respectable .364, Finley was having a good tournament, his average second only to the right fielder from Sam Houston State. After two closely-called balls, Finley hit a sluggish blooper to Norm Harding at shortstop. Norm easily threw him out at first.

Ed Griffin, the Eagle's second batter, took Ray's first two fastballs as called strikes. The next pitch was almost as on target but the rain must have obscured the umpire's vision as Ray did not get the call. With the count 1–2, however, the shortstop flew out to the waiting glove of right fielder Ron Lince.

Confidence radiated from Georgia Southern's big first baseman as he stepped to the plate with a batting average that equaled that of his teammate Finley. Intending to make a statement, Robinson's practice swings were purposeful and energetic, the bat coming to a nervous rest above his right shoulder as he waited for the windup. He went down swinging on three straight pitches.

Three up, three down. Ray had faced six batters to that point and thrown only fifteen pitches. He had successfully faced a number of heavy hitters, not only in this game but throughout the tournament, including the highly regarded Lou Brock, Southern University's lightning fast right fielder.

11:
Off Speed

Played on Wednesday, June 8, the Southern game was Whitworth's third nightcap of the tournament, starting well after 8:30 p.m. As long as Whitworth kept winning, they played in the "feature game" of the day, which was always last. It had become a ritual of sorts. It was no wonder, then, that other rituals developed during Whitworth's week in Sioux City. Every night after the game, the team would return to the dormitory, shower, change into their street clothes and head back into town for some dinner. Since the dining hall on campus was always closed by that time, the team adopted the Chesterfield, a comfortable, inexpensive diner that was close to Soos field, for their postgame meals. They had walked into the Chesterfield for the first time after 11:00 on Monday night, having just beaten home town favorite Morningside. All eyes were turned towards them as the eighteen ballplayers entered the restaurant. It was obvious that at least some of the late-night diners had come from the baseball game. Whatever reservations they might have had about entering "enemy territory" were quickly dispelled by the friendly, good-natured greeting they received. Giving the Pirates their dues, the consensus opinion was that since Morningside was now "out of the running," they might as well root for Whitworth to win the whole thing.

From that point on the entire team felt welcome. The wait staff and restaurant manager seemed genuinely pleased to see them arrive, especially when they continued to arrive victorious. The Chesterfield became Whitworth's "lucky diner." Every night they ate at the same place, sat at the same tables, and picked the same menu items, Coach Merkel included. No one ate dessert, a practice that had started at the tournament banquet on Sunday night. Every night was carefully orchestrated to be identical to the last one, even going so far as to play the same tune on the jukebox—not the latest Elvis single or the Everly Brothers but the remake of a lively old country tune called "Mule Skinner Blues" that had been recorded by the rockabilly duo known as The Fendermen. There was no sense jinxing the flow of the tournament. It was going too well. Even the waiter got in on the act, declaring, "I know the order. I'll put it on," when the team came through the door. The only exception had been the Friday before the championship game, when Whitworth had a bye, waiting for the winner of the Georgia Southern vs. Southern University play-in game. Coach Merkel, Coach Wittenburg and Ray Washburn went elsewhere to enjoy a nice steak dinner at the expense of a Major League scout who wanted to discuss Ray's "future." But the balance of the team was undeterred—their ritual dinners were sacrosanct.

Ken Wittenburg was twenty-three years old and the oldest member of the team aside from Coach Merkel. He had received his bachelor's degree from Whitworth in 1959 and returned this year to serve as the assistant baseball coach. Ken was raised in Spokane, attending North Central High School. Money was tight when he decided to attend Whitworth, requiring Ken to work several jobs in order to stay in school. He took every chance he got to earn extra money. He had been a four-sport athlete in high school, but time and work forced him to make a difficult decision and limit his athletic participation to one sport. Baseball was it. He liked Coach Merkel and baseball's season fit in best with his varied work schedule. Summers were spent at a lumber mill, and most holidays and school breaks found him supplementing his income at the post office. Ken was used to hard work. The fact that it took five years to complete one degree program and another two to get his teaching degree did not deter his resolve. Ken's work ethic and

Bill Trenbeath sliding in. *Photo credited to Don Murphy, photographer, Sioux City, Iowa.*

determination were surely attributes my father valued in his assistant coach, despite his relative youth.

Coach Merkel treated him as he would have treated any peer, conferring with Ken about game situations, potential plays, pitcher changes, and so on. This didn't necessarily mean that Coach didn't already have an idea what he wanted to do, and no doubt would have done it anyway, but he was intent on using these occasions as teaching tools, so he always made the effort to include his assistant in the decision-making process. During the tournament, Coach Merkel also made sure Ken attended all of the coaches meetings arranged and requested by NAIA officials. So when the Major League scout offered to take Coach Merkel and his prized pitcher to dinner, Ken was included in the invitation. It was an evening and an honor Ken would long remember.

In the Southern game, Ray dominated from the beginning. The strain of throwing fastballs in the first game had taken its toll on his arm, making it noticeably sore, so against the Jaguars he mixed up his pitches, with curve balls, sliders, and an occasional breaking ball thrown in to keep Southern's hitters on their heels and save his arm. The Jaguars had been anticipating their matchup with Washburn since his start against Morningside. Many of them had been in attendance at that game, wanting to get the full measure of their prospective opponents.

Southern was housed on the floor above Whitworth in the dorm. The morning after the Morningside game, third baseman Dean McGuire ran into a couple of the Southern players in the stairway, who were talking about Ray's pitching. Wide eyed with admiration, they talked about his speed and wondered out loud if they would have to face him at one point in the tournament. With their worst fears realized, it was little wonder that they were caught off guard by the mix of pitches he was throwing their direction. But this also captured the attention of the Major League scouts, who already knew about Ray's fastball and were now equally impressed with his ability to effectively throw off-speed pitches.

Of course, Whitworth team members were fully aware of Southern's prowess, not only from witnessing their pre-tournament warm-ups but also from catching the end of one of their early games. What stood out was their speed, always their speed. As they watched from the stands, Jim Glennon remarked that it was a sure bet they would steal if they got on base. With his typical audacity, Tom Ingram's retort was, "First, they've got to hit us."

Ray handcuffed the defending NAIA Champs, limiting their heavy hitters to just four hits, all singles, and recording an impressive sixteen strikeouts. This was all the more remarkable because Southern was listed as eleventh best among all college baseball teams that season by *Collegiate Magazine*, a well-known national publication. Sam Houston State, which Southern had beaten the day before, was listed as sixteenth in the nation. But on this particular day, in Sioux City, Iowa, senior Ray Washburn dominated Southern's bats. At the end of nine innings, only two pitches had been hit out of the infield—a single that worked its way to shallow left field in the first inning and a fly ball to right in the seventh. The Jaguar's star slugger and base runner, Lou Brock, struck out three times! The joke among Whitworth players was that they never even got a chance to see how speedy he was because he never got on base.

Farrell Romig broke out as the hitting hero for the Pirates in the Southern game. He was only a home run away from hitting for the cycle and in the process knocked in five RBIs. Ray capped the game off by driving in a run in the ninth inning after Norm Harding singled and stole second base. Ray's double sent Norm scampering home and ensured that his batting average remained over .300.

The final score of the Southern game was 7–0. At the midway point of the tournament, Whitworth was the only unbeaten team remaining. Pirate pitchers had fanned forty-eight batters in three full games of play. Over twenty Major League scouts were in the stands for that game alone. Ray's stats for the game included 144 pitches, 86 of which were strikes. For the big right hander, it was an impressive display.

12:

On The Board

With mist settling a little heavier over the field, the bottom of the second inning got underway. Whitworth sent first baseman Jerry Breymeyer to face Georgia Southern's Mims. With the championship game on the line, the Eagle pitcher meant business, taking just enough time between pitches to set his stance before letting the pill fly. Jerry went down swinging on three straight fastballs. But with catcher Denny Rieger at the plate, Mims momentarily lost control of his delivery, nailing Denny's left leg.

Denny limped to first base, shaking out his leg to relieve the pain. Being a catcher, he depended on his legs to carry him up and down out of his crouch smoothly, easily, and quickly. Any stiffening of his muscles at this point could prove disastrous. He settled uncomfortably onto first base, for a short time letting his mind wander back over the Pirate's baseball season and to their early trip to Seattle when certain disaster had turned into good fortune.

***

The Pirates were on their way home after disappointing and lopsided losses to the University of Washington when the generator on Rieger's 1956 Dodge, conked out on the eastern down-slope of Snoqualmie Pass. Fortunately the car stopped running close to the turnoff into Easton, a small community west of Ellensburg. But it was Saturday evening, a time when most businesses had already closed for the weekend. Relief pitcher Bob Huber was traveling behind them and stopped his car to offer assistance.

Bob came to Whitworth from Los Angeles, California. When he was a junior in high school, he attended a church summer camp where the youth director happened to be a former student body president at Whitworth. He spoke to Bob about attending college in Spokane and planted the seed. Thereafter Bob continued to do his own research on Whitworth and decided it would be a good fit for him. His sister attended college in the Los Angeles area, where it was not uncommon to be among 2,500 fellow students in one English class. That was not at all what Bob wanted; he wanted manageable class sizes, a chance for one-on-one interaction with professors, and he wanted out of LA. When his baseball team won the city championship, Bob contacted Coach Merkel. Never one to dissuade a prospective student from attending Whitworth and playing for his team, my dad encouraged him to come to Whitworth but let him know up front that there wouldn't be a lot of financial help from the baseball team. However, as was his practice whenever possible, Dad kept at it and managed to scrape together $400 in scholarships which came from the combined resources of both the basketball program and the baseball program. In 1959, that was a fair amount of money, and for Bob, it was frosting on the cake.

Bob often volunteered his car for road trips, so it was not surprising that it was Bob who stopped to offer aid to Denny and his hobbled vehicle. It was decided that Bob would use his car to push Denny's into Easton. Unfortunately the bumpers of the two cars did not match up very well, so centerfielder Lee Archer and infielder Dean McGuire sat on the hood of Huber's car, adding just enough weight to force the front end down into a more workable matchup with Denny's rear bumper. Ostensibly, to keep from injuring themselves, the two hood weights held their legs straight out in front of them for the entire ride into Easton. The strategy worked fairly well; however, sitting on the hood of a moving car presented some balance challenges, and Lee took a tumble off the hood as they limped into town, bruising his hand as he caught his fall.

Not surprisingly, the first establishment they encountered that was open for business happened to be a tavern. A helpful patron pointed to a house down the street when they heard the ballplayer's plight. While the others got some food, Denny made his way to the designated house, stepping cautiously onto a rotted wooden porch. Caution only went so far, and at one point he actually put his foot through one of the floor boards. However, the man inside was not only sympathetic but also extremely generous. He got his work clothes back on and took Denny and his disabled vehicle down to his repair shop. The mechanic had to take the engine apart and regrind a couple of valves, but he accomplished the necessary repair work as quickly as he could and finally sent the ballplayers on their way with a modest $25 tab and a slightly bruised centerfielder.

***

Denny's momentary reverie ended with a chuckle, as he realized that his leg, though painful, was going to be fine. They had come too far and been through too much to let a little thing like a goose-egg on his calf stop him. Hands on his knees, he waited as Mims readied himself to face the next Pirate batter.

Whitworth's left fielder Farrell Romig was having a pretty good tournament himself and stepped to the plate sporting a .333 batting average, third best in the tournament. Demonstrating his prowess, Farrell connected with Mims' second pitch, sending it deep into right field for a double. In the meantime, Denny had taken a lead off first and, proving that his leg was indeed fine, ran smoothly around second, settling in at third.

Runners were at second and third when Ron Lince stepped up to the plate. He glanced quickly over to third base. Once again Coach Merkel was walking away from home plate with his hands in his back pocket, hitching up his pants. This time there was no question. The base runners were ready for the squeeze bunt. With the count 3 and

1, Ron squared off at home plate, as Mims sent his fastball directly at him. Thrust instinctively into a defensive posture, Lince stepped back to avoid being hit, sliding awkwardly in the mud, the bat still square across the plate but closer to head height than chest. Miraculously bat and ball connected, sending a perfect dribbler towards first base. Mims came off the mound quickly, only to slide on the wet grass of the infield while trying to field the ball. A little dazed that the ball had even been hit, he took several seconds to realize that he was still on his knees behind home plate and that Denny was only steps from reaching home. Ron was easily thrown out at first when he finally did get up and moving, but not before, bad leg or not, Denny had scored the first run of the game and Romig had advanced to third.

The dampness in the air and on the field made it imperative to keep the equipment as clean and dry as possible. The home plate umpire kept balls in his pockets and made every effort to send dry balls back to the pitcher. But with third baseman Dean McGuire at the plate, one of Mims' pitches got away from the catcher, allowing Farrell to scamper home for Whitworth's second run. Dean eventually struck out, but with the second inning in the books, Whitworth was on the board while Georgia Southern remained scoreless.

13:
Delay Called

By the top of the third the rain had become more than a mist, making the field a little wetter, though still playable. The infield was just starting to generate small puddles of mud, the area around home plate resembling a barren isthmus jutting out from the infield grass, surrounded on three sides by standing water. The outfield was damp enough to grab a ball and hold onto it, should a grounder make it out that far.

Georgia Southern's lead-off batter was their right fielder, one of four Eagle hitters with a better than .300 average. But with the count 1–1, Stipe hit an inconsequential grounder to Norm Harding, who easily threw him out at first. At catcher, Tommy Howland had enjoyed some hitting success against Whitworth pitchers in their earlier matchups. Against Ray, he was caught looking at a called strike three. As Washburn gathered himself for the next batter, Mims, the pitcher, strode to the box. Mims was a good hitter in his own right, but in their first tournament outing against Omaha University, Mims had been hit by a pitch and spent Monday night in the hospital. Fortunately, he recovered with no lasting ill effects. However, this at-bat against Washburn was no contest. Mims swung and missed on three consecutive fastballs. The top of the third was over just that quickly, with an economy of effort on Washburn's part. He had thrown only ten pitches.

The Pirates were back to lead-off hitter Bill Trenbeath. After working Mims to a full count, Bill hit a soft grounder right back at the pitcher who had no trouble fielding the ball and throwing him out at first. Lee Archer showed considerably more patience during his second at bat, working Mims to another full count before going down swinging. With two out, Norm Harding came to bat and swung hard at the very first pitch, connecting with the ball and sending it past the infield for a single. Unfortunately, Washburn was unable to advance Norm, as he hit a pop fly to the third baseman for the third out.

At the end of three innings it remained Whitworth 2, Georgia Southern 0. But the rain could no longer be ignored, and the wind had kicked up. After a brief confab, the umpires called for a rain delay.

There was little else to do now but wait. To pass the time teammates alternately paced back and forth in the dugout or huddled on the benches trying to stay loose and as warm as possible. A couple of kids, little leaguers themselves by the looks of their jerseys and undeterred by the elements, approached the dugout looking for autographs. Jim Glennon pointed in the direction of Ray and Norm, advising the awestruck boys that they would never hear of the rest of the team again but that those two were the ones who were going to make names for themselves.

Other than that brief interlude, there wasn't much talking. It was hard to know just how long this delay would last or whether the game could even be resumed. Most of the upper classmen wore their leather-sleeved wool letter jackets, which were heavy enough to provide the warmth they needed. However, sophomore Tom Ingram had yet to receive his jacket, having just earned it at the end of the regular season. He was making do with the long-sleeved wool shirt he always wore underneath his jersey and a light wind breaker. Captain Jim Glennon generally caught for Tom when he was on the mound and was well aware that he might be asked to pitch during this crucial game. Foregoing his own comfort, Jim insisted that Tom wear his letter jacket so the pitcher could stay as warm as possible.

***

Jim Glennon was not just the Captain of the Whitworth baseball team; he was their inspirational leader as well. Even as a freshman, he was voted "Most Inspirational," an honor he keenly appreciated and strived to live up to. Jim came to Whitworth from the tiny hamlet of Emmett, Idaho, where his father was a Baptist minister as well as trainer and assistant coach at Emmett High School. Reverend Glennon was instrumental in securing a football scholarship for Jim to attend Whitworth in 1957. Jim had grown up in Emmett and had never been to Spokane prior to driving in that first day as a college freshman. It was the first time he had ever even seen a one-way street, let alone tried to find his way around a "big city." He headed for the tallest building he could see, which just happened to be St. Al's Cathedral. He had landed on the doorstep of Gonzaga University. Eventually he made his way further north to the Whitworth campus and settled in.

Like most of my Dad's ballplayers, baseball was Jim's second sport. He started playing left field as a freshman but the position of catcher was a weak spot on the roster, and when the regular catcher flunked out of school the following year, Jim stepped into the catcher's role. It was a good fit. He was not particularly fast, but he was intelligent and could get up and down out of his stance with surprising agility.

During Jim's sophomore year, Whitworth's baseball team was not very good. Ray Washburn had left to spend a year at a Junior College back in Pasco, and Tom Ingram had not yet arrived. Pitching was poor; hitting was worse. But when Jim was a junior, Ray returned to the team, Tom Ingram entered as a freshman, and Denny Reiger also arrived. Denny was a capable catcher and got some quality playing time during his freshman year. That was 1959, when they won the Evergreen Conference title outright but had to decline a trip to the NAIA Tournament because of money constraints.

14:
The Huddle

The Pirates had become a close-knit group over the course of this season, as evidenced by Glennon's selfless gesture. But it hadn't always been that way. They were a diverse group of young men. Some of them came from staunch Christian families and were devout followers of their faith. One or two might have been considered renegades when it came to some of the more conservative aspects of life on a Christian campus. There were the partiers, the academically astute, and those more academically challenged. As a result, it was no wonder that tensions arose when, after winning their first game against Seattle Pacific, they lost the next five games of the season, including losses at University of Washington, Washington State University, and University of Idaho. Team members looked forward to testing their prowess against the larger universities. Wins would have given them much-sought-after bragging rights. Losses injured their pride as well as their win-loss record. No one felt that more acutely than did Ray Washburn. The frustration of missed opportunities and sloppy play rose up after their losses in Seattle, and he had been harshly critical of his teammates, calling them a bunch of bush leaguers. That one rashly spoken remark had deeply wounded his fellow teammates and had added fuel to the animosity that had begun to overtake the Whitworth baseball team that spring.

Among team members there was a good deal of individual talent beyond Ray Washburn and Norm Harding. Tom Ingram was proving to be a strong second starter behind Ray, and Farrell Romig's bat always seemed to rise to the challenge of the best pitchers the team faced. But through the first part of the season there wasn't much in the way of mutual support and encouragement among team members. In fact, after Coach Merkel regained his health and resumed his coaching duties, he could not help but notice how much bickering was going on.

As he waited for his strength to return, my father guided the team's spring practices from a portable aluminum lawn chair that he perched in center field. My mother would drive him to the field every day, returning to pick him up again two hours later. It may have hurt his pride a bit to resort to sitting through those spring practices, but from this strategic locale he was given an excellent vantage point from which to guide their drills and observe team dynamics. One afternoon, Tom Ingram and Ron Lince got into a shouting match, with others loudly voicing their opinions as well. It was too much. One of the things Coach Merkel knew and appreciated about the game was that baseball is a team sport. One or two good athletes, no matter how exceptional they might be, were not going to win baseball games all by themselves. And so he gave the team an ultimatum: have a team meeting before tomorrow's practice and sort things out or prepare for a very long, mediocre season.

Members of the Whitworth Pirate baseball team took their coach's directive to heart and met in the college chapel for a couple of hours before their next practice. Something happened that day. Led by team captain Jim Glennon, they talked about their selfishness and suggested ways they could keep their individual egos in check while encouraging each other to do their best. Everyone contributed and everyone benefited. From that point on teammates learned to appreciate each other's individual abilities and contributions to the team. They had found the key, and a team was born. Not only did they start winning games, but Coach Merkel was able to mix up room assignments and car assignments when they traveled. Conversations became deeper and more meaningful in all respects. As the personal and individual interaction and respect grew between teammates, so too did the unification of their baseball team. They found themselves playing better and having fun.

They found more ways to get on base, made timely hits, and executed defensive plays that saved the game.

With their newfound camaraderie and easiness, teammates were also able to joke around with each other more often. During one game, utility infielder Don Cox was a runner on second base when slugger Norm Harding came up to bat. Don didn't play regularly and was not the fastest base runner. He was, however, a bit of a comedian and well-liked by the entire team. Norm hit a pretty decent single into near right field and Don advanced to third base, content to remain there. At the end of the inning Norm was obviously put out that Don hadn't tried to score. With a sly look in his eye, Don replied, "Well, if you think I am going to let you get ahead of me in RBIs you're crazy." The outrageousness of the statement was so obvious that they all had a good laugh.

It was that easiness coupled with concentration and attention to the fundamentals that successfully carried Whitworth through the balance of their season and up to this point in the tournament. And they were having fun.

Coach Paul Merkel on first base foul line with NAIA official prior to start of championship game. Ray Washburn is warming up in the foreground. *Photo extracted from 8 mm film of championship game taken by Harold McCracken, father of utility second baseman, Jerry McCracken.*

Coach Paul Merkel and Georgia Southern Coach J. I. Clements at home plate with umpires exchanging batting orders. *Photo extracted from 8 mm of championship game taken by Harold McCracken, father of utility second baseman Jerry McCracken.*

Ray Washburn warming up before the championship game. *Photo credited to Don Murphy, photographer, Sioux City, Iowa.*

Home plate stands out as an island amidst the mud and standing water about midway through the championship game. *Photo extracted from 8 mm of championship game taken by Harold McCracken, father of utility second baseman Jerry McCracken.*

Whitworth Pirates return to dugout at the end of an inning.
*Photo extracted from 8 mm of championship game taken by Harold
McCracken, father of utility second baseman Jerry McCracken.*

Jerry Breymeyer trying to beat the throw. *Photo credited
to Don Murphy, photographer, Sioux City, Iowa.*

Coach Merkel supervising the call at third. *Photo credited
to Don Murphy, photographer, Sioux City, Iowa.*

Tom Ingram throwing off the mound during championship game.
Photo credited to Don Murphy, photographer, Sioux City, Iowa.

Ray Washburn receiving Tournament MVP trophy
from NAIA official, June 11, 1960. *Photo credited to
Don Murphy, photographer, Sioux City, Iowa.*

Ron Lince and opposing pitcher "hitting the dirt" following a
squeeze bunt that drives Denny Reiger in from third to score.
*Photo extracted from 8 mm of championship game taken by Harold
McCracken, father of utility second baseman Jerry McCracken.*

Whitworth Pirates after victory against Georgia Southern. *Photo credited to Don Murphy, photographer, Sioux City, Iowa.*

Coach Merkel accepting championship plaque from NAIA official. *Photo extracted from 8 mm of championship game taken by Harold McCracken, father of utility second baseman Jerry McCracken.*

Team appreciation plaque presented to Coach Paul Merkel,
June 11, 1960. *Photo courtesy of Barbara Merkel Bell.*

15:
Uniform Misfits

When the umpires walked up to the dugout to announce the resumption of play, thirty-two minutes had elapsed. Coach Merkel and Ken Wittenburg immediately conferred with Ray as the ballplayers picked up their gloves and started warming up, tossing balls back and forth or jogging up and back along the first base foul line. To say they looked ragged might be considered kind.

Thirty-two minutes had not been long enough to even begin to dry out or soften the cloying nature of the Pirate's sodden uniforms, which were looking as old and bedraggled as they actually were. The fact that the uniforms were 100 percent wool ensured both their durability and their longevity. In fact, when asked, any one of the Pirate baseball team might have concluded that their uniforms were roughly 9,000 years old. Whether the uniforms had once been new was a question no one asked. Chances were pretty good, however, that while they probably did not date back to the Stone Age, they undoubtedly dated back to the beginning of Whitworth's renewed baseball program, making them roughly twelve years old. Their longevity eliminated any hope of being fashionable or up to date. Their durability eliminated all hope of "looking pretty" out on the field. Although Whitworth's school colors were crimson and black, the uniforms were a nondescript gray—again, very utilitarian and easily worn, whether Whitworth was playing as the home team or the visitor. On championship Saturday, those same gray uniforms looked even worse, the sweat, mud and grime of four days building into the fabric. There were no laundry facilities available to them, and so the players donned uniforms every day that not only smelled ripe but could easily have stood up on their own.

Because of their age, the uniforms tended to be impossibly baggy, especially in the pants. The jerseys fit a little better. Most of the players chose uniforms that were a little too large so they could move around in them unrestricted. That strategy worked well enough until it rained or the wind blew. In the rain, the wool lost its shape and drooped even further around their ankles. Belts were a vital accessory. In the wind, well, in the wind they might as well not even try to run. The pants tended to hold them back like a parachute on the end of a dragster.

Bill Trenbeath was fortunate enough to live with his aunt and uncle during his sojourn at Whitworth. The Eliases were Whitworth boosters and well known to Coach Merkel. As an added bonus, Dorie Elias was an accomplished seamstress, and she took the time to tailor Bill's uniform so it conformed to his body and fit more like it should have. Bill's uniform was the envy of his teammates, and on days when he did not play, there was a lottery to decide who got to wear his uniform.

It may have been, however, that these ugly, ill-fitting uniforms actually gave Whitworth an unexpected edge over their competitors in the NAIA tournament that year. The wool uniforms, while unfashionable, were made of natural fibers which made them generally "breathable" and naturally water resistant. Other than a light turtleneck, players didn't need to wear extra clothing underneath to stay warm and dry, unlike teams from the south, who seldom played in such inclement conditions and must have felt more restricted by the added clothing they were forced to wear beneath their uniforms. Besides, the weather conditions in Sioux City weren't any worse than the conditions Whitworth encountered throughout most of the season.

***

During their last series with perennial Evergreen Conference rival Central Washington College in Ellensburg, the wind was worse than usual, blowing with sustained gale force gusts clocked at 30 mph and peppered with occasional rain squalls. The baseball diamond was situated such that the wind blew straight out from home plate and directly into the face of the pitchers. Tom Ingram, a bulldog of a competitor, was on the mound during the nightcap of their double-header. The force of the wind in his face made it impossible for him to wear his contact lenses, and so he simply gathered himself and threw as hard as he could in the area of home plate, hoping that the ball would get somewhere close to the strike zone. Just steadying himself on the mound had been a challenge as the wind threatened to interfere with his balance every time he got ready to throw. Fortunately, the umpires showed some compassion and, bowing to the conditions faced by both teams, announced that if a pitcher started his motion and then got thrown off balance by a wind gust, no balks would be called.

But it wasn't just the pitchers who had experienced difficulties with the wind and rain that day. The baggy Whitworth uniforms made base running almost impossible, the wind pulling at the billowing pant legs and holding speed to a minimum. Jerry Breymeyer tagged a pitch and sent it sailing, the wind catching it and carrying it so far out that it was called an inside-the-park homerun. But in the process of running the bases, Jerry pulled a hamstring going around second and was barely able to limp home. Struggling to run inside those uniforms was a contributing factor. It was the same problem in the outfield. Hitters were having a field day. Like Jerry's homer, any balls that were hit tended to sail, and outfielders felt like they were slogging through dense gelatin trying to chase down fly balls.

Whitworth won both games in that crucial series in Ellensburg. The score of the final game was 19–16, but Tom was as proud of that performance as if they had won it 1–0.

16:
In Relief

The wait had been long, the air damp and cold. Not wanting to risk any injury that might jeopardize Ray's potential Major League career, Coach Merkel elected to go with Tom Ingram in relief and send Ray out to right field so they could still have access to his bat. Ingram was fearless, not one to get nervous when he was pitching. He had a job to do, and that was to win games. His attitude mirrored Coach Merkel's: if he did his job and the others did theirs, then they would win. If not, they would lose. Tom did not like to lose.

***

Having come to rely on Tom as a starter throughout the season, no one on the team questioned the decision to send Tom to the mound. He had been a bit of a hot dog when he arrived at Whitworth, his confidence taking on an aura of cockiness that initially rubbed teammates the wrong way. He claimed that he could throw "all pitches" and never seemed to stop talking. Eventually, it became too much for Norm Harding, especially after the significant losses at UW and WSU. Being one of the team's only two married members, Norm was hoping to parlay his skill and a successful baseball season into the chance to play semi-pro or even professional baseball during the summer and after graduation. He was deadly serious about baseball, and he had had enough of Tom's swagger. Norm threatened to really let him have it. But Jim Glennon, ever the peacemaker, offered a solution. He approached Tom with a proposition. Tom could keep talking and no one would say anything to him, as long as he kept winning ball games. But as soon as he lost just one game, he had to stop with the bravado. The deal was struck. And Tom never lost another game the rest of the season; in fact, he even pitched a perfect game that year against Eastern Washington, a feat that probably did not get the attention it deserved.

***

Under normal circumstances Jim Glennon would catch when Tom was pitching, but this time Coach wanted Denny Rieger to stay behind the plate. His rationale was simple. Had Jim come in to catch and something happened to make him unable to play, then Denny would not be able to re-enter the game, leaving them without a catcher. The Pirates simply did not have the depth to risk it. Both Jim and Tom agreed without reservation. For his part, Denny was thrilled to stay in the game and although he hadn't worked a lot with Tom, he was sure they would manage. When he was "on," Tom could pitch with the best of them. He had a good fastball, a dinky curve ball that consistently kept batters and sometimes even his catcher off balance, and an occasional knuckle ball—nothing Denny couldn't handle behind the plate. Before play resumed, Jim's only advice was a reminder for Denny not to catch Tom the same way he would catch Ray. Tom did not have Ray's power, but he did have good control. His pitches were almost always right on target. As Jim liked to say, he could probably have made the call, stuck out his mitt, closed his eyes, and Tom would have hit the catcher's mitt. High praise coming from his senior catcher.

***

At the beginning of the year, Jim, a senior with more catching experience, had been Ray's catcher while Denny, still a sophomore, had been behind the plate for Tom and Spike. However, during that first disastrous road trip to the coast, Ray made some uncharacteristically caustic remarks about team members, and Jim had retaliated, "Well, you haven't signed a contract yet." He knew instantly that he had hurt Ray's feelings, and that troubled Jim. He and Ray were roommates and friends. He didn't want anything to create a wedge in that friendship. It was Jim's thought that the team and their friendship would be better served by letting Denny catch for Ray and Jim would take over the duties for Tom. Tom's braggadocio often irritated other teammates. Jim could handle that. Ray tended to be more high strung and needed a catcher who would not be afraid to pull him up short if the need arose, would not take any guff, and would get the best out of Ray. Denny could do that. Their coach concurred and the switch was made. It worked like magic. Thereafter there was never any friction between a pitcher and his catcher, nor between the two catchers. They were doing what was best for the team and for each other.

Sophomore catcher Denny Rieger came to Whitworth from Ritzville, Washington, a small farming community about 55 miles west of Spokane. Interestingly, Denny's family had moved to Ritzville several years before from Scotland, South Dakota, where his father was a well-respected minister. Scotland residents still remembered Rev. Rieger, and once they discovered that Denny was his son, they made a point of phoning him with news of the tournament as it progressed, even before Denny could make his call. One of the gas stops the team made on their way across South Dakota was in Yankton, located just 30 miles from Scotland. Team members couldn't resist and used that opportunity to ask anyone they happened to come upon if they knew "Dennis Rieger from Scotland?" No one did, but the team got a big kick out of giving Denny a hard time and trying to embarrass him.

***

As Tom readied himself to face Georgia Southern's leadoff hitter at the top of the fourth, he couldn't help but remember the last time he faced this same team. He'd lasted only two innings, and they had scored four runs off of him. It was time for redemption.

Adjusting his cap lower over his forehead, Tom took a moment to give the rubber a kick and glance at his teammates behind him. They were already in position, focused and ready to go. They had his back. As he turned to face home plate, their chatter started and Tom went to work.

Not having had as much time to warm up as he usually did, Tom got off to a rocky start and walked the first batter he faced. Next up was the centerfielder, Rowe, who tagged Tom's first pitch for an easy single, advancing the base runner to second. With no outs and two men on, Eagles' co-captain Bill Mallard came to bat. Tom was beginning to get into his pitching rhythm and by bearing down, threw two straight strikes, both of which caught the batter looking. Behind in the count, Mallard swung hard at the next pitch, connecting solidly, rolling it up the middle, just out of Tom's reach. Norm Harding had taken position just off second, and it looked as though the ball would surely keep going into the outfield for a base hit. But luck was on the side of the Whitworth Pirates that day, much as it had been throughout the tournament. The ball actually careened off second base, right into Norm's waiting glove. Completing an unassisted out at second, Norm wheeled and made a precision throw to first, converting what might have been a base hit into a double play. With two outs and a runner now on third, Tom faced the heavy hitting left fielder, Finley. Working the count to two and one, Finley slapped the next pitch into center field and directly into the waiting glove of Lee Archer to retire the side.

It wasn't just Ray Washburn's arm that had cooled off during the rain delay; Ray Mims was no longer pitching for Georgia Southern, the Eagles sending Clyde Miller to the mound in relief. Pirate hitters proved that they were not immune to the effects of the delay either. Leading off, Jerry Breymeyer could manage little else than whiffing on three straight pitches. Denny Rieger also succumbed to the thirty-two-minute hiatus and went down swinging on three straight pitches. Farrell Romig, whose bat was normally so dependable, worked Miller to two balls and two strikes before sending a fly ball out to right field for the final out of the inning. The score stood at Whitworth 2 and Georgia Southern 0.

17:

Bases Loaded

By the top of the fifth inning the cool, damp air was beginning to take its toll on everyone. Play was getting a little sloppier, pitches lost some of their luster, and reflexes were slow. Georgia Southern sent their shortstop to the plate to face Ingram. Tom's first pitch slipped a little when leaving his grasp, arriving at home plate uncomfortably up and inside; enough so that Griffin dropped quickly to one knee to escape being hit. Standing back in, Griffin let the next two pitches sail by for called strikes. With the count 1 and 2, he popped up to Dean McGuire at third for the first out.

***

Dean McGuire was a typical two-sport athlete who came to Whitworth because of family ties. A particularly strong basketball player in high school, Dean was an integral part of a winning team in Colorado Springs, Colorado. Unbeknownst to Dean, his mother meticulously kept track of all newspaper articles written about him and his basketball team and sent copies to his brother Dick, who was already a student at Whitworth. Dick, in turn, showed the articles to Coach Hintz, the basketball coach at Whitworth, talking him up as much as possible until finally Coach Hintz offered Dean a scholarship. As was the case with many of his teammates, baseball was Dean's second sport.

***

Eagles' first baseman Robinson stepped up and caught Tom's first pitch with a solid shot towards Norm Harding at shortstop, demonstrating his hitting prowess. The ball seemed to stop dead as it hit the muddy base path, and Norm was unable to get a good handle on the ball, muffing his off-balance throw to first and putting a man on base. It was an uncustomary error for the normally efficient Harding. He was disgusted with himself. But if he had glanced over at Coach Merkel in the dugout, he would have received an encouraging clap and a "That's OK. That's OK." While stressing total concentration during a contest, Coach could accept physical errors if they were hustling type errors. He had no patience for losing focus, not following the ball when it was hit to you, not knowing what you were going to do with the ball once you got it, not knowing who had a base covered or indecision in catching a fly ball. He played to get ahead early and keep the lead with sound defense and pitching. He demanded that his pitchers throw strikes and that the rest of the team play aggressively behind him. That Norm was hustling in less than ideal conditions was perfectly acceptable.

Right fielder Stipe, another .300 hitter, was up next. Swinging full out on Tom's first pitch, Stipe hit the ball into the gap in left center for an easy single, advancing Robinson to second.

Bearing down, Ingram faced catcher Howland. As Howland approached the plate, my father suddenly loomed outside the first base dugout, his demeanor agitated, all the while proclaiming loudly, "I don't know, I don't know, I don't know." Just as he had so many times during the season, he repeated that mantra over and over, ten, twelve times in a row, a reminder to his Whitworth defenders to be ready for a bunt, hit and run, or attempted steal. With the call 1–1, Howland proved the accuracy of Coach Merkel's alarm, laying a bunt down directly in front of the Pirate catcher. However, Reiger bobbled the ball and was unable to make a good throw to first, loading the bases.

Ingram was undeterred. Despite a valiant effort, Miller, the Eagles' reliever, was unable to get a piece of the ball and went down swinging for the second out.

Lead-off man and second baseman Moody came to the plate, two out and the bases loaded. He watched the first ball zip by for a called strike one. Ingram pocketed the return from his catcher and without hesitation let loose with another throw across the plate for strike two. His third pitch missed the mark, rebounding out of the softened dirt in front of home plate and sending a shower of mud into Denny's mask as he lurched forward to block its trajectory and save an unearned run. Taking a moment to spit random shards of grit out of his mouth, Denny handed the ball to the home plate umpire who replaced it with a clean, dry one from the pouch inside his chest protector. With the bases loaded, every Pirate was at full attention waiting for Tom's next pitch. When it came, Moody hit a short pop fly to Norm Harding who deftly snagged the ball in the webbing of his glove, not about to let another one get past him. And that was it for Georgia Southern and their scoring opportunity: the side retired with three men still languishing on base.

The relief on the face of every Whitworth ball player was evident as they emptied the field in anticipation of their turn at bat. As they neared the dugout, their pace abruptly slowed in deference to the mud and standing water that had begun to accumulate in front of the dugout. Even with a bit of tip-toeing, it was still difficult to navigate the area without further saturating their shoes and pant-legs. Gathering in the dugout they took their places with waiting teammates, relief giving way to relaxed smiles. Tom's pitching was holding strong and confidence radiated throughout the dugout.

***

There was a looseness and relaxed atmosphere among team members that day, an atmosphere that had not been there during the first couple of games in Sioux City, when jitters caused occasional, uncustomary sloppy play. Even Norm Harding, perennially focused and serious, had loosened up during the tournament. During that first game against Georgia Southern, when Coach Merkel had strode to the mound to talk with Tom and his catcher, Don Cox, who was playing second base, edged toward Jerry Breymeyer for a nervous chat. Don could feel his muscles tighten, tying his stomach in knots. This was his first tournament start and the game was gut-wrenchingly hard-fought and scoreless to that point. As they stood together, Norm jogged up to meet them with a smile on his face, perhaps sensing their tension

"Isn't this fun?" he asked. "This is what we came here for—to compete against the very best. Let's just enjoy every minute."

He meant it, and just that easily Don and the rest of the team began to relax and enjoy the experience too.

Norm's looseness might have been at least partially attributable to the "game" he devised during the long afternoon hours spent waiting to get to Soos Park for their games. Rabbits proliferated on the Morningside campus, particularly around the dormitories. One of Whitworth's speediest players, Norm had made a game out of chasing a rabbit or two around the premises, using the activity not only to warm up but to challenge his dexterity and see if he could actually catch one of the critters as it darted right and then left, just out of Norm's lunging grasp. He never did catch one, although every day he swore he was gaining on it. It was that playfulness that permeated the team as they sat on the dugout bench, waiting for the bottom of the fifth to commence. They were comfortable in this setting of achievement in the face of adversity, unexpected by those who still watched in the stands but totally expected by those who played on the field.

***

Ingram led off in the bottom of the fifth, with McGuire on deck. After working his opponent to a full count, Tom was given a pass to first when Miller couldn't get the call on ball four. McGuire, Whitworth's big third baseman, stepped to the plate. The grass and the balls were wet and unpredictable. After watching three straight errant pitches, McGuire couldn't hold back, making contact with the ball and sending it right back to the pitcher, who made the easy out with a little flip to first base. Ingram advanced to second on the fielder's choice.

Bill Trenbeath was anxious to advance Tom to third and maybe get on base himself. He again worked Miller to a full count before taking a called strike three. There were two down at this point, with Ingram still holding at second base. Center fielder Lee Archer connected squarely with Miller's second pitch, but only managed to hit an inconsequential dribbler towards the mound. His reflexes already on high alert, Miller was off the mound and already bare-handing the ball before he'd barely taken two steps. Eying his prize briefly and gripping the ball securely in his hand, Miller turned towards Archer who was sprinting down the base path, and secured the third out with a confident lob to first.

The fifth inning was in the books with Whitworth still holding on to a 2–0 advantage.

Bill Trenbeath in earnest discussion with umpire. *Photo credited to Don Murphy, photographer, Sioux City, Iowa.*

18:
The Stretch

There was a general excitement rustling along the Whitworth bench as they watched their teammates take the field for the top of the sixth inning. The game was going as well as anyone could have hoped and the rain, while unrelenting, was light and playable. Daylight would be fading soon, however, so it was imperative to play at least two more full innings.

19:
Honoring Their Own

At the back of the dug-out, out of sight of Coach Merkel, was a special package that Jim Glennon and several others had picked up just that morning from the local sporting goods store. On Tuesday afternoon Coach Merkel had taken a few of them to that same store to replace the two bats that had been broken during their game with Morningside and to replenish the package of baseballs that had been lost in the canyons of South Dakota. It was unusual to have more than one broken bat in a single game. However, Coach Merkel believed that it was important that each ball player have his own glove and his own bat, one suited to his individual requirements. On this occasion, Don Cox was the recipient of a new bat picked out especially for him. Coach told him the bat would carry him through the tournament, and it did.

A day later, after they had won their second game, Don and Jim Glennon, Norm Harding, and Denny Rieger used their off hours to return to the sporting goods store to order two special plaques. Every member of the team had contributed what they could for the purchase of these plaques. They intended to present one to Ray Washburn as the team's Most Valuable Player. The other would be presented to Coach Merkel at the end of the tournament to express their appreciation for their coach's belief in them and for instilling in them the desire and belief that they could win as a team. Although no one would have considered him a brilliant strategist, Coach Merkel was nevertheless a real student of the game and, more importantly, he knew how to get the best out of each player, instilling loyalty and trust amongst all of his student athletes. The team loved him and wanted to win for him. The anticipation was sweet.

20:
Coach's Prowess

As Tom completed his warm-up pitches, Eagles' center fielder, Rowe, stepped into the batter's box. Showing considerable patience, Rowe took strike one and then watched four consecutive pitches miss the mark for Ingram's second walk of the game. With Rowe on first, Mallard's hard luck at the plate continued, and he went down swinging on three straight pitches.

Heavy-hitting left fielder Finley took a called strike one, then managed a sharp single into right field, advancing Rowe to second. With men on first and second and only one out, Georgia Southern's shortstop, Charlie Griffin, strode to the plate. Normally willing to feel out a couple of pitches first, this time Griffin got a little over anxious at the plate and immediately hit into a fielder's choice, safely landing on first while Finley was forced out at second on the throw from Ingram to Norm Harding.

There were two down and runners at the corners as first baseman Robinson stood in against Ingram. This at bat became a real duel. Robinson worked Tom to a full count, fouling off several inside curve balls before finally flying out to Norm Harding at shortstop. Once again Georgia Southern ended the inning, stranding base runners in scoring position with no runs to show for it.

Whitworth players cleared the field, trotting back to the dugout with ever increasing confidence. Coach Merkel was making his way to his normal position in the third base coaching box. Generally unflappable during games, some tension was beginning to show on his face. He never seemed to have a lot of highs and lows during a game, his demeanor remaining constant whether the team won or lost. Although there were occasional "discussions" with an errant umpire or two, they were few and far between, Coach Merkel preferring to let the game play out as it would and trusting his team to make the plays needed to win the game. But this time, it was evident that he really wanted them to win, more for the sake of his players than for his own.

***

The first time I ever witnessed one of my father's "discussions" with an umpire, I was barely eight years old, sitting in the meager stands loosely constructed behind home plate, my mother and sisters beside me. I instantly came to attention, my eyes wide, a knot tightening in the pit of my stomach. Coach Merkel was vigorously disputing a call, his red face inches from the umpire's mask, his Roman nose jutting forward with every word. At that moment Coach Merkel was no longer a coach… he was my dad … and with the reasoning of a child, I was sure that the man behind the mask had committed some unpardonable sin and therefore deserved my father's ire. Not understanding the full gist of his display, I was nevertheless nonplussed to see the blue man's thumb suddenly jerk upwards and out. Just as suddenly, my father's assistant coach stepped forward and led him to the dugout. I was confused. Where did he go? Why was someone else suddenly standing where my dad belonged in the third base coach's box? I clutched my mother's skirt as I watched the display, my anxious fingers seeking reassurance as they curled tightly in the fabric, the chaos in my mind much more dramatic than the actions on the field. She calmly explained that Dad had been thrown out of the game for arguing with the umpire. Thrown out of the game? The man in the blue suit had thrown my father out of the game for standing up for one of his players; for pointing out what must have been an obvious error in the man's judgment? I was indignant and clearly ready to be mad at that umpire for the remainder of my young life. Which might have been the end of it had I not seen my father and that very same umpire chatting like two good friends immediately following the game, my dad casually resting his hand on the blue man's shoulder as they shared a laugh. Later my mother confessed that Dad and Ed (blue suit and all) had extended their conversation over coffee at Ferguson's Café, our family favorite! To my uninitiated mind, my father's fraternization with such an enemy was tantamount to an act of treason.

That my father truly cared for each one of his players was never in doubt, to me or to anyone else who saw him in action, either on the field or off. He treated coaching as if it were his personal and moral duty to champion his athletes, whether it be in the face of a questionable call of an errant umpire or the miserly budget allotments of a small college athletic department. More than that, he respected his players both as athletes and as individuals. He rarely raised his voice at someone more than once, allowing his athletes to make their choices and then live with the results. It was an effective character-building technique. In return, the ballplayers wanted to play hard for him. I remember my mother holding dinner on many occasions while we waited for Dad to get home from "the office." He loved talking to his players and would stay at his office, which was little more than a hole in the wall, poorly lit, windowless and lined with bookshelves in the basement of Graves Gym, for as long as anyone needed him to. It didn't matter if they wanted to talk about baseball or about school or about life in general; he was there for them and they knew it.

What they hadn't fully realized up until the tournament was the level of contribution Coach Merkel had made to the NAIA organization since its very inception. He was nationally recognized and had served as president of the fledgling NAIA Baseball Coaches Association; but he seldom spoke about himself or his own accomplishments, preferring to concentrate on the accomplishments of his players and those around him. Even at home I seldom recall my father speaking about his leadership positions with national organizations or his own awards other than when he gave a requested interview to local sportscasters or newspaper reporters. He served because he believed in the organizations and wanted to further the national prominence and interest in college athletics, especially amateur baseball. For those organizations to which he belonged, he worked tirelessly, no small feat considering the amount of time he spent with his duties at Whitworth … not only as baseball coach, but also as Athletic Director and Sports Information Director, although at the time this was not a specific compensable position in the athletic department.

At this point in the history of Whitworth athletics, Sports Information Director entailed work that simply had to be done if Whitworth was to be acknowledged with more than a passing paragraph in the newspaper or on the TV/Radio. In my father's mind, Whitworth's athletes deserved much more than an afterthought on the evening news, and he went out of his way to nurture a personal relationship with local newscasters and sports writers, building his credibility as well as his cadre of friends and supporters. Each night my father would forego sleep to compile statistics and game highlights to wire back to the two Spokane area newspapers, the *Spokesman Review* and the *Spokane Daily Chronicle*. When he could he would also place a call to Dick Wright, a radio sportscaster who had become a personal friend and always made room in his broadcast for news from the tournament. It was through the paper and Mr. Wright that we at home garnered any real information about the events taking place in Sioux City. The cost to place a long-distance call was prohibitively expensive, so phone use was necessarily restricted. As did many of Whitworth's supporters, my mother was relegated to sending a short, thoughtfully-worded telegram to Dad and his team to express our pride in their accomplishments on the field.

However, any thoughts that Coach Merkel's abilities in the sport he loved were limited to administrative activities were effectively dispatched one day at practice. They were fooling around a bit towards the end of practice and several team members had cajoled Coach into standing in the cage and taking some cuts. He had never done anything like that before. But this time he did and proceeded to hit line drive after line drive. The entire team was suitably impressed that he could just step in without any practice and hit the ball with such consistency. If they ever doubted his prowess before that day, they never did again.

21:
Standing Guard

Coach Merkel was set up at third base. Miller had completed his warm-up pitches and was ready to face Whitworth's first batter, Norm Harding. After one ball and one strike, Norm connected for another single and headed to first base. With a man on base, Ray Washburn stood in to face Miller. When Ray was relieved of his pitching duties, he had been sent out to replace Ron Lince in right field. Although a solid hitter in his own right, Ron's batting average did not match Ray's and in this game, every hit, every run, counted.

***

Ron Lince was easily the largest athlete on the Whitworth baseball team, standing a good three inches above Ray in height. Ron began his baseball career at Whitworth as a catcher, battling with Jim Glennon for the premier catching slot. He was also a tackle on the football team and was enrolled in officer training school. During the summer following his freshman year, Ron attended Marine boot camp. If his size was formidable before that summer, it was particularly imposing after he returned from boot camp. He was significantly bulked up and muscular, which, while impressive, did little to enhance his abilities as catcher. Lacking the flexibility to pop easily up and down out of his catcher's stance, Coach Merkel reassigned Ron to right field and designated Jim Glennon as starting catcher.

Being the most physically imposing member of the team, Ron also earned the moniker "Guardian" for his role in protecting Ray from the day-and-night pursuit of the Major League scouts at the tournament. While Coach Merkel chased off the ever-persistent Morningside coeds who were still on campus and cheerfully threatened to interfere with the purpose and focus of the other team members, Ron stood guard both in the dorm and in the dugout against the scouts. Scouts would come down to the dugout both before and during a game and want to talk to Ray. As they brusquely pushed their way closer to their target, they would inevitably come face to face with Ron, who would bar their way with his arms tightly folded across his chest and firmly tell anyone, no matter who they were or what organization they were with, that, "Ray has more important things to think about than your conversation. Just leave him alone until it's over." There was no doubt that he meant it.

Although Ray and Jim Glennon normally roomed together, at Morningside, it was Ron who bunked with Ray, and for good reason. On one or two occasions scouts actually tracked Ray down at the dorm, knocking at their door at 6:30 in the morning, wanting to talk about the upcoming game, how his arm was holding up, or any one of a number of topics that were repeated throughout the week-long tournament. One such morning, Ron angrily met one unfortunate man at the door and hoisted him up against the wall by his collar, making it known that the guy should get lost, that he and Ray needed their sleep. Whitworth had played the late game the day before, as they had through-out the tournament. This meant that they didn't get to bed until well after 1:00 a.m. and Ron did not appreciate being awakened by anyone, especially by a scout who had been previously warned to stay away. They were not bothered again in the early morning hours.

***

With the championship game on the line, Ron was only too willing to make way for Ray in the outfield, ready to add his vocal support from the dugout as Ray stepped to the plate. Ray had already flied out twice and wanted desperately to smack one out of the park. After a called strike and another swing and a miss, Ray managed only to send a sluggish ball toward the third baseman, who bare-handed it and lobbed a throw to second base for the forced out.

Jerry Breymeyer took two well-placed pitches by Miller before hitting into what should have been a fielder's choice; but the throw to second was too late to get Washburn, and both runners were safe. With runners on first and second, Denny Reiger walked on four straight balls, loading the bases for Farrell Romig.

***

Farrell Romig was a sophomore. He had grown up in Spokane and played baseball at North Central High School. A highly-recruited left fielder, as a freshman, Farrell accepted a hefty baseball scholarship to play at Pacific Lutheran University in Tacoma. Prior to entering PLU, Farrell had already attracted the attention of local scouts for the New York Yankees organization. Unfortunately, he sustained a serious knee injury during his inaugural football season and was unable to play baseball that spring. As a result, he lost his scholarship and returned home to Spokane. Fortunately for Whitworth, when his knee recovered, Farrell opted to stay in Spokane and play for Coach Merkel. Not only did he prove to be one of their leading hitters, his defensive prowess in the field was dependable and sure.

***

Romig took a called strike one before watching two balls cross the plate. Farrell was well aware of his job … hit the runners home any way you can. He swung at the next pitch, but the ball fell victim to the dampness of the infield grass, rolling without much force into the waiting glove of the third baseman. Ray had taken a big lead off third base and shot home as fast as he could, only to be cut down at the plate by a well aimed throw from the third baseman to the catcher. On the fielder's choice, Romig advanced to first base.

It was up to Tom Ingram to bring home the runners who still

loaded the bases. Tom connected with Miller's first pitch, a high pop fly that was easily snagged by the shortstop to end the sixth inning. Three Pirates were left stranded.

22:
Insurance Run

In the top of the seventh, right-fielder Stipe stepped aggressively to the plate to face Ingram for the second time. It was desperation time for Georgia Southern, but Tom had found his groove and Stipe struck out swinging on three straight pitches.

Next up was the freshman catcher, Tommy Howland, who worked Tom deep into the count before tagging a solid hit and advancing to second base with a stand-up double. At Friday night's tournament awards ceremony, Howland had been named to the all-tournament team along with teammate Tracy Rivers, who pitched against Whitworth in their first matchup, losing to Tom Ingram 1–0. Surprisingly, Ray Washburn was the only Whitworth player to be named to the all-tournament team, although he did take home the honor of the tournament's most outstanding player.

Ingram purposely took a step off the mound, pausing a moment to collect his thoughts as Eagles pitcher Miller settled in at the plate. This was no time for his concentration to waiver; and there was the little matter of regaining his bragging rights. Not about to surrender control of the game, Ingram leaned over, eyes peering out under the brim of his cap towards Denny Reiger, waiting for the signal. Meanwhile, Coach Merkel was again standing outside the dugout, loudly calling out, "I don't know, I don't know, I don't know." Over and over he repeated the phrase with machine-gun rapidity. Infielders instantly came to alert, muscles poised for action. It was an effective alarm system.

Still intently focused, Tom hurled a fastball toward the plate. Miller took an ineffectual swipe for strike one. After yet another wild swing and a miss, Miller was caught napping, watching a curve sail past for a called strike three.

With two out and a runner on second, Eagle second baseman Moody watched Tom's first pitch miss, but the next two were right on the mark for called strikes. In a last ditch effort to bring the runner home, Moody connected with a fastball and sent it sailing towards Ray Washburn, who was patiently waiting in right field. He pocketed the ball easily, successfully squelching the Eagles' hopes with another shut-out inning.

As the Pirates left the field, their enthusiasm was evident. Coach Merkel's philosophy was to play the game and enjoy it; that philosophy remained omnipresent in the team's approach to practices and to games. It was nice to win, but the enjoyment they experienced in simply playing the game might have been the key to their success at the tournament. The only expectation they had was to play hard, give all they had, and let the chips fall where they may. Winning just made it all the more enjoyable.

Yes, they were having fun, but they were ready to finish this game. Ingram was holding up well in the pitcher's spot, and the seven men behind him had supported him with efficient fundamental defensive plays. After holding the lead for five innings, the Pirates did not intend to lose.

The first Whitworth batter to face Miller in the bottom of the seventh was Dean McGuire, the Pirate's stalwart third baseman. Miller missed on his first pitch. The second one got away from him even as it left his hand, hitting McGuire and giving him a pass to first base.

***

Although this was the first time Pirate batters faced Miller in this tournament, they had watched him pitch in one of Georgia Southern's earlier games and had observed his tendency to get rattled with a man on base. Whitworth had finished practice ahead of schedule on Monday and Tuesday, and Coach Merkel let them watch the games being played just before their own. However, my Dad stopped that practice after the second night, preferring that his players keep their attention and focus on their own upcoming opponent rather than watching other teams. It also allowed team members time to relax and socialize with each other.

Whitworth's daily team practices were orchestrated to coincide with their scheduled games. Because Whitworth continued to play in the late game, their practice time was also later in the afternoon, which worked out well since they seldom got to bed before 1:00 a.m. Mornings settled into a nice leisurely pace. While Ken Whittenburg and Coach Merkel got up to scout a team they thought Whitworth might eventually face, the rest of the team slept late and were often the last into breakfast, if they made it at all. Breakfast was served during a relatively short window of time from 7:30 to 8:15 am. Lunch, however, stretched from

Ray, Tom, Dean, and Bob playing cards during down time. *Photo courtesy of Jerry Breymeyer.*

10:30 am to 2:00 pm and Whitworth team members were more likely to make an appearance then. Thereafter they would while away the hours before batting practice and infield workouts by walking around campus or town, playing cards, and writing postcards to send home. Post cards were the cheapest and most efficient way to send messages home for the money-strapped players. Dean McGuire, in particular, made it a point to send postcards to his mother. His father had died the year before, and his mother wanted him to return home and finish his college education in Colorado. A concerned uncle intervened and convinced Dean to stick it out at Whitworth. As a concession, Dean vowed to write his mother regularly during the school year. During the tournament, he wrote every day.

Generally the Pirate ballplayers just tried to stay out of trouble. It wasn't that difficult. They knew what was expected of them by their coach, their families, and their teammates. Despite the usual distractions inherent with college life, eager coeds and a new city, they acted accordingly. Not one team member broke training rules during the entire tournament, so focused were they on winning. It helped that they were bone tired after playing the late game four nights in a row, but it would have been at too great a cost for any one of them to carouse around. Basically, their tournament experience amounted to baseball, baseball and more baseball. And that suited them just fine.

***

Miller struggled with his control in the matchup with Bill Trenbeath, missing badly with his first two pitches. Jerking out of the way of an inside pitch that brushed the brim of his cap, Bill lost his balance momentarily and stepped out of the box to calm his own nerves. He firmly settled his cap forward over his forehead. Taking another deep breath and one final full-throttle practice swing, he returned to the plate and eyed the Eagle pitcher. On the third pitch, Bill couldn't hold back, bouncing the ball to the third baseman, who deftly tossed him out at first. The sacrifice advanced McGuire into scoring position at second base.

Having been on base once, Lee Archer was eager to hit the ball and get there again. Infielders were playing well up, intent on holding McGuire at second. Archer showed a great deal of patience, despite his innate desire to clobber one out of the park. He worked Miller to a full count before duplicating Trenbeath's efforts, hitting a short dribbler directly to the third baseman, who, because of his position on the field, had no other play option and made the toss to first. McGuire slid safely into third.

With two down and a runner now on third base, Norm Harding stepped to the plate. There was determination in every step he took, in every practice swing and every piercing look he aimed at the pitcher. Miller, at least a little intimidated, nervously watched McGuire at third and Norm at the plate while taking his catcher's signals. His first two pitches missed badly. But Norm wasn't waiting for the perfect pitch and swung at an outside curve ball, sending it into left field. Whether it was the field conditions or simply poor play, the left fielder was unable to corral Norm's well-hit ball. Norm rounded first base and without

Dean McGuire sliding into base. *Photo credited to Don Murphy, photographer, Sioux City, Iowa.*

109

hesitation started for second. The Eagles left fielder panicked and made a wide throw to second, taking the second baseman far enough off base and off balance to allow Norm to safely slide into second while McGuire scored from third. The bench erupted. An insurance run was enthusiastically celebrated by everyone in the Whitworth dugout! And Norm was standing at second base with heavy hitting Ray Washburn up to bat.

Unfortunately, Ray swung at Miller's first pitch, hitting a one-hopper to the shortstop, who made the toss to first for their third out. Nevertheless, Whitworth had scored another run. At the end of seven innings, Whitworth had pushed across three runs while Georgia Southern remained scoreless.

23:
Treading Water

Center fielder Rowe led off for Georgia Southern in the top of the eighth, hoping to get something started for the Eagles. He had already been on base twice, once on a single and the last time with a walk. He was intent on getting on base again. Patiently he worked Tom to a full count before taking a deep cut at a slow-moving curve ball, missing badly for strike three. With a disgusted slap to his hitless bat, Rowe slumped to the dugout.

Pinch hitting for third baseman Mallard, McMillan wasn't able to muster any kind of power, and on the second pitch he sent a pop fly to first base for out number two. All eyes turned to left fielder Finley as he stepped to the plate. Always a dangerous hitter, Finley, Tom knew, was capable of hitting one out of the park even in these adverse conditions. Tom's first two pitches missed the mark, moving well outside the plate, although one actually caught Finley off guard. Indecision might have played a role as he swung late, the ball smacking smartly into Denny's waiting glove. However, with the count two balls and two strikes, Finley hit a one-hopper to Norm Harding, who, despite Finley's speed, easily threw him out at first. Three up and three down. The scenario couldn't have been better for Whitworth. Georgia Southern was down to its final at bat, and although the rain would not relent, it remained light and play continued.

In the bottom of the eighth, Georgia Southern tabbed Pierce

Blanchard to relieve Miller, hoping to limit any further scoring opportunities for Whitworth. The few onlookers who remained in the stands huddled under umbrellas and rain gear, their perseverance a testament to a rather stubborn refusal to abandon their vigil.

Jerry Breymeyer was the first to face Blanchard. In the stands, fellow teammate Jerry McCracken's father was one of the valiant fans still firmly planted in the stands. The proud father courageously attempted to keep his 8 mm camera dry while he filmed the championship game, hoping to memorialize at least a small part of this contest for his son and the rest of the Pirate squad. The task was a formidable one. Gray clouds and the incessant rain created an impenetrable screen through which to watch the action unfold on the field, the waning light creating merely an impression of dark shapes moving around the diamond.

As Harold McCracken filmed, Breymeyer connected solidly with Blanchard's third pitch, but Georgia Southern's shortstop was able to field the ball and throw him out at first. Denny Rieger took a final practice swing in the on-deck circle before striding to the plate. Although he had been on base twice before, he hadn't yet gotten a hit. He was eager to rectify that situation. Denny settled into the batter's box purposefully, taking only a couple of half-swings before looking directly at Blanchard, his muscles tense, the bat quiet above his head. Without hesitation the catcher connected on Blanchard's first pitch, a single into right center field.

Denny was stationed firmly at first as a determined Farrell Romig took a hard cut at the first pitch but failed to connect. With the count at one ball and two strikes, Farrell watched the next pitch sail by for called strike three. Whether he agreed with the call was hard to tell. Players were not encouraged to question an umpire's call, and there was no sense in starting now. The only visible tell was Ferrell's energetic toss of the batter's helmet towards the Pirate dugout, sending it hydroplaning across the muddy expanse.

With one out and a runner on, Tom Ingram was ready to tack on another insurance run. He was a decent hitter, his season average was a respectable .300. In fact, in a mid-season game against Central Washington State College, Coach Merkel made what Tom believed was a roster error, listing Tom as lead-off hitter in the night cap of a double header. Determined to show his stuff, Tom wound up going 3 for 4 in that game. If he could do it then, there was no reason he couldn't do the same in Sioux City, in the championship game. His chance came on Blanchard's very first pitch. Tom swung with all his strength, clobbering it into left-center field for a stand-up double, allowing Denny to score easily from first base. Again the bench erupted. The sky was gloomy and gray, but inside the Whitworth dugout broad smiles greeted Denny after he tagged home plate.

Next to face Blanchard was Dean McGuire. Blanchard appeared shaken by the previous play, and there was a serious miscommunication with his catcher on the first pitch, resulting in a passed ball and advancing Tom to third base. But with the count even at 2 and 2, Dean flew out to right field, ending the inning and stranding Tom at third. At the end of eight, Whitworth held the edge over Georgia Southern, 4 to 0. Time was running out for the Eagles.

24:
Banner Raised

Crunch time. Georgia Southern was facing their final at-bats. Their uniforms, once pristine and white, had taken on a sodden gray appearance and looked almost as grungy as Whitworth's. Georgia Southern had ridden into Sioux City on a fancy Greyhound bus with new uniforms and a swagger in their steps. They represented Area 7, which included Georgia, Florida, North and South Carolina, Tennessee, and West Virginia, and were well acquainted with tournament play. The day before, they had beaten the defending champs and odds-on favorite Southern University to advance to the championship game, and they had walloped Whitworth and Tom Ingram in a game just two days earlier. They knew they could hit him. They sent their first batter to face Ingram with the intention of doing just that.

Shortstop Griffin stepped to the plate, taking Tom's first pitch for ball one. Griffin smiled. Tom glared back. Peeved, Tom stretched and used his whole body to throw as hard as he could. Griffin smacked the ball hard. Under ordinary circumstances a ball hit that sharply might have lifted past Norm Harding, waiting at shortstop, but the rain once again took its toll, and the ball languished through the grass, making it easy enough for Norm to scoop it up and get Griffin at first.

Eagle's first baseman, Robinson, pounced on Tom's first pitch, slogging into first base with a single and bringing right fielder Stipe to the plate, intent on duplicating the success he had in the fifth inning.

After two called strikes, Stipe couldn't hold back and hit into a fielder's choice, second baseman Bill Trenbeath easily tagging the runner coming into second.

Whatever applause could be heard from the stands was barely noticeable to either team. The constant gray pallor of the sky had eventually dulled their senses, shutting out color and muting any sound. The only smell down on the field was the grass, rain-soaked and muddy, and whatever lingered of the burnt gasoline along the base paths.

With Georgia Southern down to its last out, the Eagle bench held its collective breath. The Pirate bench did the same while their counterparts on the field riveted their attention on the batter at the plate. Tommy Howland had just hit a double off Tom in the seventh inning and he stepped into the batter's box with confidence. It was a classic duel between pitcher and batter. Howland worked Tom to a full count, successfully fouling off a series of pitches to stay alive, his team's last hopes resting squarely on his shoulders. Finally, on the payoff pitch, Tom's eighth of this at-bat, Howland tagged a grounder to Harding, who, just as they had practiced time and again at Coach Merkel's insistence, expertly anticipated the ball's trajectory and scooped it out of the grass, making a perfect throw to first for the final out.

Whitworth players stormed the mound, jubilantly tossing their hats and gloves into the air, back slaps resounding amidst the gray haze of rain and approaching dusk. Because of the condition of the field there would be no dug pile of players on the mound this day. Nevertheless, their joy was abundant. Victory was their reward and vindication was their prize. In wet, muddy, second-hand, 100-percent-wool uniforms, the team crowded around home plate to joyously accept the championship trophy from NAIA officials. Those who remained in the stadium bleachers at Soos Park rose and gave them a much-deserved standing ovation. Smiles were broad. My Dad, the coach, looked proud, while remaining composed, even when exuberantly lifted up on the shoulders of some of the players. He was the coach, after all. But his pride was evident and it was hard not to smile and join in with a champion's excitement.

In deference to the various media still on site and the NAIA publicity director, who wanted to complete his business and get in out of the rain, the team massed together for a group photo, their uniforms rain soaked and stained with a week's worth of mud and sweat. Their appearance did nothing to discourage the broad grins they each wore on their face.

After all the postgame awards were distributed, Jim Glennon stepped forward and took the microphone. On behalf of the entire 1960 NAIA Champion Whitworth Pirate baseball team, Jim presented Ray with the team's Most Valuable Player. The other plaque was inscribed: "To an outstanding coach—Paul Merkel." It was presented in appreciation not only for his leadership but also for his belief in every member of the Whitworth squad. The plaque included small individual plates bearing the names of all of the players on the 1960 team. The smile on my father's face as he accepted the plaque was broad, his pleasure evident.

The simple, heartfelt plaque had been paid for with hard-earned money, scraped together by each one of my Dad's ballplayers and, out of his many awards throughout the years, was his most cherished

Whitworth Pirates receiving championship trophy/plaque from NAIA official, June 11, 1960. *Photo credited to Don Murphy, photographer, Sioux City, Iowa.*

acknowledgment. As long as I can remember, except for a week or so when Jim Glennon retook possession of the plaque to add the words "1960 NAIA Champions" to the inscription, the plaque held the place of honor in our home, hanging above the living room fireplace until the day my father died. When it was finally taken down, a shadow of the plaque remained visible on the wall, a testament to the enduring memory of eighteen young men, their coach, and one unforgettable season.

Captain Jim Glennon presenting team appreciation plaque to Coach Paul Merkel. *Photo extracted from 8 mm film of championship game taken by Harold McCracken, father of utility second baseman, Jerry McCracken.*

Captain Jim Glennon presenting team MVP plaque to Ray Washburn.
Photo credited to Don Murphy, photographer, Sioux City, Iowa.

25:
Off The Hook

Once the obligatory press photos were taken, the Pirates returned to the Morningside campus to shed sodden uniforms and climb into comfortably dry street clothes. Spirits were elevated despite their fatigue. Many of them would opt to make one last visit to their lucky café, eager to share their good fortune with their new friends at the Chesterfield. They had, however, earned the right to celebrate in their own way and my father gathered everyone together in the lobby to let them know that this was their evening. They were free to do what they wished as long as they were prepared to leave early the next morning.

Before they could scatter, the mayor of Sioux City arrived at the dormitory, thankful to have caught the Pirate squad before they went their separate ways. After a brief congratulatory speech, the mayor presented them with a "key to the city." In so doing he also told them to enjoy their evening, and if they ran into any trouble that night, they were to call him and he would "fix" it for them. No doubt the offer was made in jest; however, amidst the laughter, Coach Merkel could be heard admonishing his team, "Now, boys." They had maintained a level of decorum that he did not want to see kicked to the curb now that they had walked away with the championship. No, he wanted to be sure they left Sioux City with their dignity intact. He need not have worried.

After dinner team members were "on their own" for the remainder of the evening. But it had been a grueling tournament—five games in six days—and most of the guys were beat. A couple of them took Rieger's car and opted to see a drive-in movie. Abe Roberts went bowling with Coach and Ken Wittenburg. Ray, Dean, Tom, and Ron returned to the dormitory and, unable to sleep, played double-deck pinochle until the wee hours. Whatever stroke of luck was with Whitworth that week spilled over into that pinochle game. In one hand Ron, who was partnering with Tom, laid down all twenty spades, and in the next Dean scored a double flush and racked up a 1500 run for the first time in his life. It was just the sort of miraculous occurrence that marked their entire championship run.

Bill Trenbeath decided to return home to North Dakota with his parents; it was summer break at Whitworth and there was no reason to return to campus. Bob Huber opted to accompany Dean McGuire to Colorado Springs, intending to spend a few days visiting with Dean and his family before flying home to Los Angeles. Not having their own transportation, Bob and Dean actually hitchhiked their way to Colorado. I sometimes wonder whether my father knew of their intention to hitchhike. Nevertheless, the absence of Bill, Bob, and Dean made it easy to fit Glennon and Lince in for the ride home.

26:
Home Safe

Bright and early Sunday morning, the team was up, dressed, and ready for a short breakfast before beginning their long trek back to Spokane. On close examination it was noted that Denny's car engine was suspiciously warm before they even started out that morning. But no one was talking, and it was left at that. Fatigue had settled in.

They were on the road by 7:30 Sunday morning. In their zeal to get home, team members hardly noticed that Coach let slide a church service that morning to begin the drive to Spokane.

For most of the team members, the return trip was a blur. When they weren't driving, most of them slept. My father had resumed his normal position in the lead car, where Ray did most of the driving. As was his habit, Ray was quick to pick up the pace when his coach was asleep.

Around noon they ventured into a small town in South Dakota that boasted a large smorgasbord lunch on Sunday afternoons. It seemed like the perfect place to eat their fill before continuing on with their trip. When the team entered the establishment, my father approached the proprietor and mentioned where they had been. "These guys are a bunch of big eaters," my father declared. "You might want to charge a little more per person than normal." The proprietor, although appreciative of the warning, opted instead to take the squad to a back banquet room, where all the food they could eat was wheeled in on carts. It became a contest as to who could eat the most, and the food kept coming at no additional charge. No one ever admitted to being the winner of that contest.

The opportunity to relax and enjoy a good, filling meal left everyone in high spirits. Because money was always tight, especially on road trips, the Pirate baseball players were more accustomed to Coach handing out coins from rolls of quarters in order to grab a quick hamburger and fries along the way. In comparison, this meal had been a feast. But now a choice needed to be made. They could drive back to Broadus and spend a night in the hotel, arriving in Spokane late Monday night, or they could elect to drive straight through and arrive in Spokane on Monday morning. There were enough drivers to accommodate the trip straight through, but it would be an arduous end to their already energy-draining week. There was little doubt which option was foremost in the minds of the ballplayers. They were eager to get back to Spokane. Norm Harding and Dale Roberts were both married and anxious to see their wives. Others had girlfriends waiting for them. Ray Washburn wanted to be available should a call come from one of the Major League teams who had so ardently pursued him during the tournament. Tom Ingram was anticipating news of his own from a semi-pro team in Bellingham as to whether he would be given an opportunity to play with them during the summer.

The choice was made, and the four-car caravan again took to the road. This time, no one got lost. They made several stops along the way for a quick bite to eat, but as long as they weren't driving, they usually slept. This may be why there are conflicting memories about the stops they made. Did they really venture back to that little café in South Dakota to show off their winning hardware to the tattooed waitress, or did they bypass that stop for a quicker bite at a roadside burger joint? Years later, some team members relay a vivid memory of making that stop and delighting the flirty waitress with tales of their exploits at the tournament. Their teammates just roll their eyes.

The weary travelers reached Coeur d'Alene, Idaho, early Monday morning, just before 6:00 a.m. During a brief stop, Coach Merkel took the opportunity to call someone. The team was unsure just who that was, but they assumed it was Mrs. Merkel or Coach Cutter or someone who could alert family members and make sure that the facilities at Graves Gym would be open so they could stow their gear when they arrived on campus. What they were not expecting was the police escort that was waiting for them at the state line between Washington and Idaho. All the way to campus, two Washington State Patrol cruisers escorted them into town, paving the way and creating a lot of attention. They rode onto campus with their escort still in tow to a throng of Whitworthians who had enthusiastically dropped what they were doing to be waiting for the triumphant Pirates.

More used to the obscurity of being an afterthought on page 3 of the daily sports page, the throng that greeted the young athletes upon their early morning arrival on campus was both unexpected and exhilarating. The front page of the *Spokesman Review* proudly proclaimed, "Whits Own First Title," with a picture of the team giving Coach Merkel a celebratory shoulder ride after their win. A sports writer for the *Spokane Daily Chronicle* was also in attendance that morning, waiting to secure interviews with Ray, Norm, and their coach.

Kisses, tears, back slaps and cheers resounded before my father got down to business. There was still work to be done. Gear had to be stowed, the rental car had to be returned, and calls had to be made. Two telegrams that arrived in Sioux City after their departure finally caught up to the team just before they cruised onto campus. My father didn't need to read these aloud. They were from his family, those of us who had been waiting patiently at home for news of their victory.

```
June 13, 1960 - 11:00 a.m.
To: Paul Merkel
From: Mom, Dad. Ruth, Roy, and kids
(dad's mother, stepfather, sister,
brother-in-law and their kids)

"Congratulations. We are thrilled at the
news. Wishing you a safe trip home."
```

```
June 13, 1960 - 11:00 a.m.
To: Paul Merkel
From: Irene, Linda, Claudia, Barbara and
Mother Pruter (Dad's mother-in-law)

"Congratulations from the girls at home.
We knew you could."
```

But that was not all that was waiting for the Whitworth squad. Word came that the entire city of Spokane was ready to celebrate their victory. The ballplayers were all free to go home, but it was hoped that most of them would postpone their departure for a day in order to participate in the festivities. It was unanimous. Everyone elected to stay.

On Tuesday, June 14, 1960, every member of the 1960 NAIA championship baseball team who had returned to Spokane once again piled into their personal automobiles and drove downtown, where they were greeted by the mayor and several members of the Spokane Chamber of Commerce. A local car dealership donated the use of six brand-new convertibles, tops down and ready to parade through the streets of Spokane. Three players were strategically perched atop the rear seat of each convertible as they slowly wound their way up Riverside Avenue, eventually culminating in a stop at the historic Davenport Hotel, where a full-spread luncheon was hosted by the Chamber of Commerce and the local Sports Writers and Broadcasters Association (SWABs). For the small college located on the northern outskirts of town which rarely generated much interest either in the media or with area businesses, this was indeed a special occasion.

At home on Tuesday afternoon, my father got a phone call from another sports writer who was writing a follow-up article for the evening *Chronicle.* I could hear only my father's side of the conversation, but as he always did, he downplayed his own part in the championship, preferring to bolster the team aspects of the game he loved so much. "Sure we had our stars from game to game," I heard him say, "but in the long haul it was the intense desire of the entire group that made the

Whitworth Pirates on Morningside campus proudly displaying championship banner. *Photo courtesy of Jerry Breymeyer.*

Whitworth Pirates in civilian clothes following parade in downtown Spokane, June 13, 1960. *Photographer unknown.*

whole thing possible." Later, when making a statement for the morning newspaper, my Dad elaborated, "The one thing that stood out in my mind was the attitude of the team. They went there with the idea of winning it all and then did just that. It was a complete team effort."

Perhaps he was right. Perhaps they did have the idea of winning it all, but maybe the idea of winning was just a logical carryover from the philosophy my father instilled in them from day one on the practice field. The only real expectation was that they would play hard, give all they had, and let the chips fall where they may.

Epilogue

In the long run, it was not just their championship that was remarkable; it was the bond that these eighteen Whitworth athletes forged during the 1960 baseball season that carried them to victory. That they were able to put individual egos aside for the benefit of the team is a testament to their camaraderie and their dedication to creating something singular and special. With my dad at their core, the young Pirate ballplayers transformed themselves into a cohesive unit with a shared dream, a dream that, although improbable, became a reality. The strength of that bond was so strong that it transcended time and space to remain intact years later. As Lee Archer remarked at their fifty-year reunion, "This was the best team I ever played on. We built the kind of relationship that endures throughout a lifetime."

Not everyone played regularly, but there were no duds on the 1960 team. Ray and Norm may have gained recognition as the premier all-around athletes, but the rest of the team played hard and backed them up. One or two players cannot win a baseball game. This team, with all of its individual, rather diverse members, stands as a prime example of the whole becoming greater than its parts. Without any one of those parts, the magic would have been dispelled and its power diminished. The first lesson of power is that we are all alone and the last lesson is that we are all one, connected to the greater spirit within each of us —just as it was with the 1960 Whitworth College baseball team.

That year, my father was part of something extraordinary. As his ballplayers later admitted, he may not have been a "wiz" of a coach (his strategies were basic and founded on the fundamentals of a game that has become a complex mixture of mechanics and technique), but he sure was a "wiz" of a person, and they all wanted to play their best for him. Actually, he may not have been a "wiz" of a father, either. He made mistakes, but his mistakes were not made for want of caring. Looking back on it, he provided a model for his children and his students of what it was like to realize your dreams, maybe not in the way you first imagined them but in any way life afforded you the opportunity.

As I look back at it from the advantage of age, I realize that what I perceived as neglect and deprivation was in fact a perfect lesson of strength of purpose. My father discovered the truth of who he was. He recognized his passion and had a strong sense of what his life was meant to be. It involved bringing together young men, blending their individual personal and athletic talents and creating a team, one that endured not only on the field but off the field and throughout their lives. To say they were just a group of regular guys who played with two or three gifted athletes would belie their collective accomplishment. Every member of that team, no matter how much they played, no matter how limited their role, was critical to the team's success.

Equally noteworthy is the fact that all of the ballplayers from my father's 1960 baseball team graduated from college, some going on to graduate school and law school. A great many of them eventually became teachers and/or coaches themselves. Several either played professional or semi-pro ball or participated in recreational baseball/softball leagues. Ray eventually signed with the St. Louis Cardinals and enjoyed a productive career in the majors for ten years. Interestingly enough, Lou Brock was a teammate on the Cardinals for many of those years.

Norm Harding signed with the New York Yankees and spent a couple of years with their farm clubs before an injury forced him to give up his baseball career and return to Spokane. Tom Ingram played semi-pro ball in Canada before becoming a school administrator and softball umpire. Not only was he an educator and school administrator, Don

Cox also served for many years as a state representative from the Colfax/Palouse area in Washington. In contrast, Jerry McCracken only played that one year of baseball before graduating in 1962.

I know my father was proud of each and every one of those young men. They embodied for him the core values of his chosen profession: commitment, tradition, and pride. As he wrote in a message meant for team members returning for their first reunion, seven years after winning the championship, "Very few coaches in the profession can say (and know) that they had such top individuals as athletes, who have all graduated and become an important part of the world today and who are such outstanding examples of a Whitworth graduate."

Ray Washburn pitching for St. Louis Cardinals. *Photograph courtesy of Ray and Bev Washburn.*

Win or lose, Dad loved his players. He was interested and personally involved with every one of them, not just as ballplayers but as people. He pushed and pulled some through school, whatever it took to get them to graduation. He found them jobs, scholarships, wives (he wasn't above a little matchmaking), and sometimes even their faith. He lived by example and threw himself into his life's work with rare abandon. Baseball, mentoring, teaching, and living a strong Christian faith all blended together, and few could discount his dedication to any of these aspects of his life. He was the kind of person, the kind of teacher, whom alumni wanted to see whenever they returned to campus.

Throughout his career Dad remained dedicated to Whitworth and to baseball. In his zeal to further the cause of intercollegiate and amateur baseball, he served on national boards and committees for the NAIA Baseball Coaches Association, the US Baseball Federation and the American Association of Baseball Coaches. He received numerous meritorious awards and honors for his unfailing service to the game, although he never took it upon himself to solicit recognition or "toot his own horn." Over the years he was inducted into the Hall of Fame of four national and regional organizations. Although he didn't limit his coaching to baseball, it remained his special love, his guiding force. On the diamond he found solace and fulfillment. When he wasn't coaching, he signed on as groundskeeper for the Spokane Indians, originally the Triple A affiliate of the Los Angeles Dodgers. It afforded him the opportunity to work with Tommy Lasorda, who was manager at the time, and other up-and-coming Dodger greats. Finally, when he could no longer coach, he used his proficiency with numbers to become official statistician for the entire Whitworth Athletic Department. He officially "retired" in 1990, but until his painfully bowed knees and failing health finally sidelined him, Dad remained an integral part of the Whitworth community, attending as many athletic events as possible in his ongoing role as statistician. In return, the baseball field at Whitworth now bears his name.

Fifty-year reunion of the 1960 Whitworth baseball team
members at Merkel Field, Whitworth University, May 2010.
Reprinted courtesy of Whitworth University Archives.

My siblings and I had the privilege of witnessing firsthand the kind of purpose and dedication my father exhibited every day. I may not have understood it as a child, but sometimes age casts a wiser eye on the past, both erasing the pains of childhood and elevating our memories to all that is exceptional about a parent.

My father did not diminish his family by his dedication to baseball. On the contrary, by creating a personal bond with each of his ballplayers, he expanded our core, bringing each one of them into our familial circle. I know their names and their faces as well as I know those of my aunts, uncles and cousins. Sometimes the ties that bind a family are as simple and as complex as a game of baseball.

After the 1960 Championship season my mother and father added two more children to our family, including another sister and my brother, Raymond Norman, who was named after two of the outstanding ballplayers on the 1960 baseball team, Ray Washburn and Norm Harding. My brother's link to the team was solidified at the moment he received his name.

And now, I too know my part in the championship of 1960. I am the storyteller.

Acknowledgments

I want to acknowledge with gratitude the 1960 Whitworth baseball players who answered my questions and shared, with both humor and honesty, their memories of the trip to Sioux City. That their recollections did not always coincide with one another only made for livelier discussions and heartier laughter. As one of the "Merkel kids," they allowed me to listen in on their reminiscences, their teasing jabs, and friendly banter, all of which made it possible for me to reconstruct, with a bit of "literary license," the story of their journey to a national championship. It has been an honor and a privilege to be so entrusted with their memories.

I also want to acknowledge my family, including my sisters, Claudia, Barbara and Cyndi and my brother, Ray. It is for them and future Merkel descendants that I began this project, to document the singular achievement of our father and his baseball team. It is through storytelling, after all, that we maintain our ancestral connections.

I am especially grateful for my children, Ara and Steve, who inspire me daily and who have brought into my life joy, personal growth, an ever-expanding family (Caryn, Dermot, and little Geneva Marie), and an undying respect for human perseverance and determination. I love you all immensely.

I would be remiss not to gratefully acknowledge my dear friends, all of whom have been supportive of this endeavor from the very beginning.

As they believed in my ability to complete this project, so I came to believe it myself. Thank you!

To those who so ably offered their editing assistance with both grammar and structuring suggestions, I am also extremely gratified. Your input was invaluable.

I would be remiss not to mention videographer Tom Engdahl, for his assistance in converting the old 8 mm film of the championship game to DVD and then extracting still photos from that DVD for use in this book.

And finally I wish to say "Thank you" to my friend Arnie, who opened my heart and reminded me of all that is good about the sport of baseball.

Appendix

Tournament Statistics/Summary

Georgia Southern's final championship game stats reflected a dismal 0 runs on 5 hits and 2 errors in what could only be designated as weather-related adverse conditions. They left nine men stranded.

Whitworth scored 4 runs on 7 hits, leaving eight men on base. They also committed two errors. This was Whitworth's third shutout in five games.

By the end of the tournament, the Whitworth Pirates managed to set a number of NAIA tournament records. Together, Pirate hurlers recorded 62 strikeouts in five games, a record that stood for many years and still ranks as the fourth highest in tournament history, 52 years later. Their record of three shut-outs in five games has only been matched by one other team, Lewis & Clark State College.

Ray's final stats: 37 strikeouts in three games pitched, a total of 19 full innings. Batters managed no runs and only five hits and he gave up only five walks on his way to an impressive ERA of 0.00. Ray continues to share the tournament record for fewest earned runs allowed.

Tom's final stats: Pitched in four of the five games Whitworth played for a total of 18 and 1/3 innings. He recorded 21 strikeouts and ended the tournament with an ERA of 1.5.

Spike Grosvenor earned a tournament record of his own: the most wild pitches in NAIA tournament history, with three in one game.

As far as fielding records, Denny Rieger was credited with 20 put-outs in the game against Morningside College, thus establishing a tournament record that stood until 1965, when the catcher from Carson-Newman was credited with 23 put-outs. That game, however, went 14 innings.

Whitworth's leading hitters during the tournament were Farrell Romig with a .316 average; Norm Harding, who hit .300; and Ray Washburn, who added a .294 batting average to his impressive pitching statistics.

In post-tournament awards, given out on Friday before most of the teams returned home, Ray was the only Whitworth player to make the First Team All-tournament squad and was selected as tournament MVP, based not only on his impressive ERA but on his tournament batting average as well.

All-team Honorable Mentions went to Farrell Romig, Denny Rieger, and Norm Harding.

As an interesting footnote, the summer of 1960 turned out to be the last year Soos Park housed a minor league baseball team or hosted a tournament. In 1961, the franchise was recalled by league directors and the stadium was torn down, replaced some years later by a quarter-mile motor speedway track.

Whitworth College
1960 NAIA Baseball Tournament
Offensive Statistics

Player	At-Bat	Run	Hit	2-base hit	3-base hit	Home run	Walk	Strike-out	RBI	Slugging PCT	Batting AVG
Romig	19	4	6	3	1		2	3	6	.579	.316
Harding	20	3	6	1			1	1	2	.350	.300
Washburn	17	4	5	1		2	5	5	4	.706	.294
Rieger	12	5	3				4	1		.250	.250
Breymeyer	15	3	3				1	4	1	.200	.200
Ingram	5	0	1	1			2	1	1	.400	.200
McGuire	15	2	3				2	3	1	.200	.200
Archer	21	1	4	1			3	4	1	.238	.191
McCracken	8	1	1				0	5	1	.125	.125
Lince	9	0	1				3	2	3	.111	.111
Trenbeath	9	0	1				0	3	0	.111	.111
Cox	5	0	0				1	1	0	000	000
Glennon	6	0	0				1	2	0	000	000
Huber	1	0	0				0	1	0	000	000
Grosvenor	0	0	0				1	0	0	000	000
A Roberts	0	0	0								000
D Roberts	0	0	0								000
Totals	162	23	34	7	1	2	26	36	20	.302	.210

Stolen bases:	Sacrifice hits:	Hit by pitcher:
Harding – 2	Breymeyer – 2	Cox – 1
Breymeyer – 1	Grosvenor – 1	Harding – 1
Romig – 1	Harding – 1	Rieger – 1
McGuire – 1	Lince – 1	
Archer – 1		
Washburn – 1		

Whitworth College
1960 NAIA Baseball Tournament
Defensive Statistics

Player	Put-outs	Assists	Errors	Fielding AVG
Glennon	20	3	0	1000
Washburn	17	3	0	1000
Trenbeath	2	5	0	1000
Ingram	0	5	0	1000
McCracken	1	3	0	1000
Romig	4	0	0	1000
Lince	3	0	0	1000
Cox	1	0	0	1000
Rieger	45	0	2	953
Breymeyer	22	2	2	923
Harding	11	10	2	913
McGuire	3	10	2	867
Archer	6	0	1	857
Grosvenor	0	0	0	000
Huber	0	0	0	000
A Roberts	0	0	0	000
D Roberts	0	0	0	000
TOTALS	135	41	9	952

Double plays:	Left on base:
McGuire-Washburn	Whitworth – 38
Trenbeath- Harding- Breymeyer	Opponents – 40

Whitworth College
1960 NAIA Baseball Tournament
Pitching Statistics

Wild pitches:	Passed balls:
Grosvenor – 4	Rieger – 1
Glennon – 1	

Whitworth College
1960 NAIA Baseball Tournament
Pitching Statistics

Pitcher	Games	Comp. games	Innings	Hits off	At-bats off	Runs off	Earned runs	ERA	Walks	SO	Hit batter	Won	Lost	PCT
Washburn	3	1	19	5	77	0	0	000	5	37	1	2	0	1000
Ingram	4	1	18 1/3	13	87	4	3	1.5	6	21	2	2	1	667
Grosvenor	2		4 1/3	7	26	11	8	16.0	6	2	0			
Huber	1		3 1/3	4	17	1	1	3.0	2	1	0			
Totals		2	45	29	207	16	12	2.4	19	61	3	4	1	800

1960 NAIA Tournament Scores

Southern University (LA) 3	Southern Illinois 1
Georgia Southern 4	Nebraska-Omaha 2
Sam Houston State 6	Indiana (PA) 1
Whitworth 10	Morningside College 4
Indiana (PA) 2	Southern Illinois 1
Nebraska Omaha 8	Morningside College 1
Southern University 10	Sam Houston State 8
Whitworth 1	Georgia Southern 0
Georgia Southern 5	Indiana (PA) 2
Sam Houston State 4	Nebraska-Omaha 1
Whitworth 7	Southern University 0
Georgia Southern 12	Whitworth 1
Southern University 8	Sam Houston State 6
Georgia Southern 3	Southern University 1 (Play-in game)
Whitworth 4	Georgia Southern 0 (Championship)

Line Scores – Whitworth Games

GAME 1

	1	2	3	4	5	6	7	8	9	R	H	E
Whitworth	0	0	0	1	2	1	3	1	2	10	10	2
Morningside	0	0	0	0	0	0	0	4	0	4	4	5

GAME 2

	1	2	3	4	5	6	7	8	9	R	H	E
Whitworth	0	0	0	1	0	0	0	0	0	1	1	2
Georgia Southern	0	0	0	0	0	0	0	0	0	0	3	2

GAME 3

	1	2	3	4	5	6	7	8	9	R	H	E
Whitworth	0	0	0	0	0	4	0	2	1	7	11	1
Southern	0	0	0	0	0	0	0	0	0	0	4	0

GAME 4

	1	2	3	4	5	6	7	8	9	R	H	E
Whitworth	0	0	0	1	0	0	0	0	0	1	4	1
Georgia Southern	3	1	1	0	0	7	0	0	0	12	13	0

GAME 5 – CHAMPIONSHIP GAME

	1	2	3	4	5	6	7	8	9	R	H	E
Georgia Southern	0	0	0	0	0	0	0	0	-	0	5	2
Whitworth	0	2	0	0	0	0	1	1		4	7	2

1960 NAIA Tournament
Participating Teams

SOUTHERN UNIVERSITY

Baron Rouge, Louisiana

Representing Area 5 (Arkansas, Louisiana, Alabama, Mississippi, and Kentucky)

Season Record: 21–3

Notable Statistics: Team batting average: .335; Team pitching ERA: 2.1

Defending NAIA baseball champion

SAM HOUSTON STATE

Huntsville, Texas

Representing Area 2 (Texas, Arizona, Colorado, New Mexico, Utah and Oklahoma)

Season Record: 21–9

Team Pitching: Leading pitcher gave up only 10 hits in 72 innings during season. Pitcher #2 gave up only 13 hits in 86 innings.

Notable wins during the 1960 season: Big Ten Champion Minnesota

One of the 1960 NAIA Tournament favorites

OMAHA UNIVERSITY

Omaha, Nebraska

Representing Area 3 (Kansas, Nebraska, North Dakota and South Dakota)

Season Record: 21–3

Notable Statistic: Team batting leader maintained a .426 average

Runner-up to Southern University in the 1959 NAIA baseball championship

SOUTHERN ILLINOIS UNIVERSITY

Carbondale, Illinois

Representing Area 6 (Illinois, Indiana, Ohio and Michigan)

Season Record: 16–6

Notable Statistic: Team batting leader maintained a .566 average throughout 99 plate appearances

GEORGIA SOUTHERN UNIVERSITY
Statesboro, Georgia
Representing Area 7 (Georgia, Florida, North Carolina, South Carolina, Tennessee, and West Virginia)
Season Record: 17–9–1
Notable wins during 1960 season: Kentucky, South Carolina and Florida State

INDIANA STATE COLLEGE
Indiana, Pennsylvania
Representing Area 8 (Pennsylvania, New York, New Jersey, Maryland, Washington DC, and "New England")
Season Record: 12–3

MORNINGSIDE COLLEGE
Sioux City, Iowa
Representing Area 4 (Minnesota, Wisconsin, Iowa, and Missouri)
Season Record: 15–4
Host School for 1960 NAIA Baseball Tournament

WHITWORTH COLLEGE
Spokane, Washington
Representing Area 1 (Washington, Oregon, Idaho, California, Nevada, Montana, and Wyoming)
Season Record: 13–7

Whitworth's 1960 Baseball Team
Regular Season Results

April 1, 1960 – Away
- Whitworth vs. Seattle Pacific Falcons.
- Rain-abbreviated game – 6 innings only.
- Whitworth won 10–5. Spike Grosvenor was the winning pitcher.
- Later that day they played a practice game that Whitworth lost 3–2.

April 2, 1960 – Away
- Whitworth played a double-header against University of Washington.
- Lost first game 15–1. Ray Washburn was losing pitcher.
- Lost second game 14–12. Tom Ingram was losing pitcher.
- Much of the problem stemmed from errors committed by Whitworth players.

April 6, 1960 – Away
- Whitworth traveled to Idaho for a game against Idaho Vandals.
- Whitworth lost 6–3. Spike was losing pitcher.

April 9, 1960 – Away
- Whitworth travelled to Pullman for a double header against WSU Cougars.
- Whitworth lost first game 1–0. Ray Washburn had thrown a 4-hitter, but the game was lost on an unearned run.
- Whitworth won second game 2–0. Tom Ingram was winning pitcher holding WSU to 2 hits.

April 16, 1960 – Home

- Start of League play.
- Whitworth played double header against Central Washington College of Education.
- Whitworth won first game 4–0. Ray was winning pitcher, holding Central to 5 hits and striking out 8.
- Whitworth won the second game 7–2. Tom won that game. He had 11 strike outs and no walks.

April 21, 1960 – Away

- Whitworth played at Gonzaga.
- Whitworth lost the game 12–2. (Newspaper report was sketchy and did not name losing pitcher.)

April 23, 1960 – Away

- Whitworth played double header against Eastern Washington College of Education.
- Whitworth won the first game 4–3. Ray Washburn was winning pitcher.
- Whitworth won second game 2–0. Tom Ingram was winning pitcher. No hits, no runs, and no one reached base. Tom threw only 70 pitches. It was a perfect game.

April 30, 1960 – Home

- Whitworth played double header against Eastern Washington College of Education.
- Whitworth won opener 7–0. Ray Washburn was winning pitcher on a 4-hitter. Also hit a homerun and drove in 4 runs.
- Whitworth took the second game 4–0. The last three games of the series were shut-outs.

May 3, 1960 – Home

- Whitworth played Gonzaga.
- Tom Ingram was pitching and led 3–1 when the game was called on account of rain.

May 7, 1960 – Home
- Game scheduled against Larson Air Force Base team.
- Cancelled on account of rain.

May 10, 1960 – Away
- Whitworth played Gonzaga.
- Whitworth won 6–2. Ray Washburn was winning pitcher with 10 strikeouts.

May 14, 1960 – Away
- Whitworth played double header at Central Washington.
- This was for the Eastern Division championship of the Evergreen Conference.
- Whitworth lost the first game 5–4 Ray Washburn was losing pitcher—his first league loss.
- Whitworth won the second game 19–16. Tom Ingram was winning pitcher. This game was wind aided, blowing 25 mph.

May 17, 1960 – Home
- Whitworth played Gonzaga.
- Whitworth won 5–2. Ray Washburn was winning pitcher. Threw a 2-hitter.

May 20 and 21, 1960 – Away
- Evergreen conference Play-offs played at Pacific Lutheran University.
- Whitworth played double header. Whitworth won first game 8–0. Ray Washburn was winning pitcher and threw a 1-hitter with only one walk.
- Whitworth won the second game 6–1. Tom Ingram was winning pitcher. Threw 5-hitter.

All-conference honors

All-conference shortstop: Norm Harding
All-conference outfielder: Farrell Romig
All-conference catcher: Jim Glennon
All-conference pitchers: Ray Washburn and Tom Ingram

After conference title and in preparation for NAIA tournament, games were scheduled on May 28, 1960, with Fairchild Air Force Base. These games were practice only and were not reported.

However, scores were: Whitworth 17–1
                                  Whitworth 13–1
                                  Whitworth 11–1